P9-CKH-648

street gang awareness

A Resource Guide for Parents and Professionals

STEVEN L. SACHS

Fairview Press *Minneapolis*

Published by Fairview Press, 2450 Riverside Avenue South, Minneapolis, MN 55454.

Library of Congress Cataloging-in-Publication Data
Sachs, Steven L., 1953–
Street gang awareness: a resource guide for parents and professionals / Steve Sachs.
p. cm.
Includes bibliographic references (p. 224) and index
ISBN 1-57749-035-5 (pbk. : alk. paper)
1. Gangs—United States. 2. Juvenile delinquency—United States, Prevention. I. Title.
HV6439.U5S23 1997
364.1'06'60973—dc21 97-2963
CIP

First Printing: June 1997
Printed in the United States of America
01 00 99 98 7 6 5 4 3 2

Cover design: Circus Design
Cover photograph: © 1996 Circus Design Inc.

Publisher's Note: Fairview Press publishes books and other materials related to the subjects of social and family issues. Its publications, including *Street Gang Awareness,* do not necessarily reflect the philosophy of Fairview Health System and its treatment programs.

For a free current catalog of Fairview Press titles, please call toll-free, 1-800-544-8207.

To my beloved family—

past, present, and future.

Train a child in the way he should go: and when he is old, he will not depart from it.

—Prov. 22:6

Contents

Acknowledgments

First and foremost, I want to offer my profound thanks to Fairview Press and to my publisher, Ed Wedman, who saw the importance of this book and took a chance on a new author.

I would like to thank my editor, Lane Stiles, who gave me not only encouragement, but also structure to my text, drawings, and photographs. His results are the finished copy you see today. All writers should be so lucky. A dinner in Highwood is on me at the Nite N' Gale.

Thanks to my copy-editor, Debbie Bihler. Her red pen, copious notes, and thoughtful suggestions allowed me to pause, sit back, and rework the text so the reader could better understand it. Special thanks to editorial assistant Stephanie Billecke for patiently answering questions as well as asking them. I tip my hat.

Many thanks to all the people behind the scenes at Fairview Press who helped breathe life into this book.

I especially want to thank my wife, Pepper, and my daughter, Lindsay, for putting up with the entire project. They unselfishly gave me time to write, time that was rightfully theirs.

My gratitude to Officer Steve Jones of the Waukegan Police Department, who allowed me to photograph part of his Nazi memorabilia collection, items he uses to educate students on the atrocities of the Holocaust. Thanks to Tony Quinn—colleague, gang expert, friend. To my friend and colleague, Frank Sebesta, an unbelievably great musician and songwriter whose humor has helped brighten many a day, thank you. Need I say more? To my friend Rob Reisener, who has given much encouragement along the way, an SNC among the sea of ordinary chondrites. Many thanks.

Many thanks to Chief Raymond Rose and Commander Keith Kalodimos of the Mundelein Police Department, who allowed me and my camera access to their collection of confiscated gang paraphernalia. My gratitude to the Los Angeles Sheriff's

Department for sharing essential information, and to fellow officers who graciously allowed me access to the many mimeographed handouts given to them at various gang seminars these past years.

Thanks to Mr. Ronald Stephens of the National School Safety Center for the use of his Gang Assessment Tool, and Matthew S. Moore, publisher of *Deaf Life,* for his valuable assistance in locating the American Sign Language illustrations used in this book.

Finally, I am grateful to the many gang and ex-gang members and their families who cannot be thanked by name, but who trusted me enough to share their lives, experiences, and insights. Their contributions added greatly to this book.

AUTHOR'S NOTE

This work is not an official publication of the 19th Judicial Circuit or Lake County Court Services. The opinions and views given herein are those of the author and may not represent the position of the 19th Judicial Circuit or Lake County Court Services.

Introduction

The year was 1978. I was just beginning my career in corrections as a counselor at a detention center for juveniles. Nintendo was some years away. Children with pocket pagers were unheard of. Young parents were trying out the latest disco steps to the beat of the Bee Gees and Barry White. That was the year the rumors began, rumors of gangs forming in the northern suburbs of Chicago. Some community leaders and police officials were unwilling to acknowledge the presence of gangs. But juvenile probation officers and detention counselors, as well as youth officers among police departments' rank and file, saw a different scenario. It was no rumor. The gangs weren't just migrating north from Chicago—they were already here. The violence had begun.

Move ahead seventeen years.

It was a sunny July day in 1995. I walked out into the waiting area adjacent to the courtroom of the juvenile courts building where I worked as a probation officer. Mr. Williams and his son Jerome* were just coming out of the courtroom. Jerome was now officially off the house arrest program I helped supervise. I shook hands with Jerome and Mr. Williams, wishing them both well. My supervision of this young man, and approximately seventeen others like him, involved frequent phone calls and a daily home visit while he awaited his court hearing. Jerome was an honor student in science at the local high school. Because I am also interested in science, Jerome and I had several engaging conversations about the topic. Jerome was bright and articulate, and looked forward to going into the field of science.

He was also charged with a criminal offense. Rather than lock Jerome up in the already crowded county juvenile detention center, the judge released him to the custody of his parents and our program.

*The names have been changed.

Sentenced to two years' probation, Jerome followed our house arrest conditions. It was good to see him do well; his future looked a bit brighter. I said good-bye to him at 4:10 P.M.

Less than two hours later, Jerome lay dying in his girlfriend's arms, his blood surging out onto her blouse from gunshot wounds to the head—a victim of a drive-by gang shooting. His life flickered out in seconds.

Sadly, this same scenario is played out a number of times every day across the nation. Did Jerome's parents know that he flirted with gangs? I knew he did. It was my job to know. Even though Jerome was not a gang member, he associated with other young men who were. As the worn-out saying goes, Jerome was "in the wrong place at the wrong time."

Parents have always watched in terror and amazement as the children they raised faced life's decisions. However, today's decisions are harder-edged, more high-tech, and infinitely more dangerous. Our children will decide whether or not to become involved in gang activity, and this decision will profoundly color the outcome of their lives.

Back to my original question. Did Jerome's parents know he associated with gang members? They knew Jerome associated with "questionable" types, kids they really didn't approve of. Jerome's parents both worked full-time, which frequently meant long hours. Short of camping out on the front lawn to keep an eye on Jerome's nocturnal activities, they couldn't possibly have kept him away from his friends twenty-four hours a day.

Jerome was the oldest of three children. Now he was the first of their children to die. Had the Williams done everything they could to steer Jerome away from gangs?

Quite possibly they didn't see the signs. What signs? Maybe Jerome's friends had the strange habit of wearing identical baseball caps cocked to one side. Perhaps they were seen around the neighborhood with one pant leg riding a little higher than the other. Maybe Jerome's friends all sported beautiful, gold Star of David pendants around their necks. Were they all Jewish?

This book is written for all the Williamses of this world. It doesn't matter whether your name is Smith, Sanchez, Goldstein, or Fong. Children are dying. Young people are killing other young people, and innocent bystanders as well. Today's promising youths are becoming tomorrow's local headlines. This book is a reference tool for parents, educators, and anyone else who wants to know what to look for in a child who might be involved in—or experimenting with—gang culture. It also explores the recourses communities and individuals may take to combat the spread of gang activity.

I am not a therapist. I have worked with delinquent juveniles and gang members since I began my counseling career at a juvenile detention center in 1978. What I have seen in the lives of these young people over the years is truly frightening.

A street gang is a structured, cohesive group of individuals, usually between the ages of eleven and twenty-five, who generally operate under some form of leadership while claiming a territory or turf. Gang members wear distinctive clothing, use special street names and symbols, and commit organized, spontaneous criminal acts within the community. Gang members may be male or female, rich or poor, white, black, Asian, Hispanic, or any other group.

We often consider gangs to be a problem of the inner-city, and at one time this was true. Today, however, smaller cities and towns are becoming the home turf for gangs and victims of gang activity. This is no accident. There has been a steady migration of inner-city gang members to sleepy suburbia, the result of either their parents' housing or job relocation, or their desire to expand their drug trade. Now, more than ever, smaller police and sheriffs' departments are having to educate themselves about gangs and reevaluate their anti-gang strategies.

Many suburban law enforcement agencies now employ full-time gang officers to patrol schools and communities. New gangs are forming every week, and youths are joining up at an alarming pace. What's more, older gang members are now having children, and these children are themselves becoming enmeshed in gang life: the cradle-to-grave syndrome.

I'm pulling no punches in this book. Breaking this cycle will take a supreme effort among educators, law enforcement personnel, and families. Many parents, educators, and law enforcement officials will disagree with my opinions or methods or both. Some might even question why I would write a book that young people could look at and "get ideas from." My reply is, simply, this: "Hogwash!" Today's youths are sophisticated. Most will already recognize much of the material presented here. Why shouldn't you be armed with knowledge that the majority of youths already possesses?

The key person here is you, the reader. Whether you are a parent from the increasingly rare nuclear family, a single parent who must go it alone, or a relative who has put your own life on hold to help raise the child of another family member, you are your child's role model. Sports figures, actors, musicians, and political leaders are unrealistic role models, at best. At worst, they are fleeting, disappointing, and even harmful. Your child does not live with Michael Jordan or Mother Teresa. Nor does he or she live with Mike Tyson or Madonna. Your child lives with you.

As parents, we cannot just sit back and watch gangs and society raise our children. We must become involved. An informed parent is a better parent. Get involved with schools, youth organizations, churches, neighborhood watches. Read the latest literature concerning gangs, especially those in your area. Learn the slang. Contrary to the impression they give, kids feel frustrated when the adults in their lives are ignorant and uninformed about teen subculture. It is a primary cause of strained communication—the generation gap, as we have come to know it.

Signs of gang activity are all around us. From the symbols kids draw to the clothing they wear, the signs are there. The signs have always been there. We have known what to look for all along.

But more important is what we, our children's caretakers, decide to do about it. We could look the other way and deny that our children are involved with gangs. If we're lucky, we won't get that police visit to our home, or that dreaded call from the hospital. Maybe we won't have to face the same stark reality Mr. Williams and his family were forced to endure.

That kind of ignorance is dangerous. Time is not on our side. If we don't take a proactive approach in addressing gang issues with our children, gangs will have the upper hand. Children as young as seven and eight years old are already trying to emulate older gang members. They are making adult decisions at a non-adult age. The consequences of these decisions may last a lifetime.

When you discover that your child may be in a gang or experimenting with the gang lifestyle, what do you do? Fair question. Tough answer.

There are a number of resources available to parents today, from communities, schools, police, churches, and neighborhoods. Much of this help was unavailable only a few years ago. Today, all you have to do is ask. But ask loudly. Check with school officials and police and probation departments. City government and youth organizations are also good sources. The fourth section of this book contains many ideas and possible resources to help get you started.

Again I must emphasize the word *you*. You. You. You. You are the key here. If you're telling your children you're concerned about them out of one side of your mouth, while blowing marijuana smoke out the other, put this book aside and read it later. Your children will be looking at you. Note that I say, "at you." They may not be looking *to* you for help or guidance at this time, especially if they are older teenagers. But your children will be observing what you do. If you have any self-destructive habits, now is the time to work them out.

It's not going to be easy. Most studies show that the family is the first line of defense in fighting gang activity. Conversely, these same studies show that the family can be the number one factor that pushes a child toward a gang. Either way, the family seems to have the most significant effect on which direction a child takes.

But keep one thing in mind. Despite everything that families do to steer their loved ones away from gangs, sometimes they lose the battle. That's a painful thought. Prisons and state juvenile detention facilities are filled with gang members who were once preteens. If you know in your heart that you have tried every trick in the book, left loving lines of communication open and offered sound direction for your child, then it may be time to face the reality that your child has made a conscious decision to join a gang despite your efforts. Face it, peer pressure is a powerful thing. Gang pressure can be even more powerful. Add to that the regressive elements of today's youth culture—music, movies, and videos that promote violence, and a trend toward ever earlier self-destructive behavior, such as drug and alcohol abuse—it's no wonder we sometimes lose the battle.

Some years back, I worked with a fifteen-year-old gang member who was housed in the local juvenile detention facility. One day we had a conversation about gangs. He boldly stated, "I've decided that crime is what I want to do the rest of my life. My life belongs to the gang." When I pressed him for details, he continued. "I'm willing to lose my freedom if I get caught. So what? They can't lock me up forever. Why should I work at a crummy fast-food joint, flippin' burgers for chump change, when I could go out and steal a woman's purse, and get, maybe, fifty or a hundred dollars?" A smile flickered across his face as he concluded, "Five minutes of work. All tax-free!"

This young man justified his future crimes with simple but twisted logic. At the tender age of fifteen, he had already made a willful decision to stay with the gang and continue his criminal lifestyle. Despite a number of community-based services given him, including probation and residential treatment, he always gravitated back to his gang. I followed this young man's criminal career over the years, and true to his word, he's now doing his third stretch at an adult penitentiary in Illinois.

Enough doom and gloom. I sincerely hope you, the reader, will discover preventative strategies before your child has the chance to become involved with a gang. If, after reading this book, you find your child displays none of the gang indicators, count yourself lucky—for now. If your child is already involved with a gang, there are steps you can take to confront the issue and possibly reclaim your loved one.

This book is the result of hundreds of hours of professional training, in conjunction with many thousands of hours of work with delinquent juveniles, current and former gang members, and their families. Additional research from regional and nationwide law enforcement agencies supplements my personal experience with gangs. In my research I discovered many books on gangs, all containing generalities, statistics, and narratives written in the first person. But none provide the information parents and caretakers need most: how to determine whether a child is involved in a gang.

The information provided here has never been available to the public—until now. But why should professionals be the only ones with access to this information? It's you, the parents and educators, who must face the reality of gangs day in and day out.

This book will cover only the most well-known gangs in the United States, focusing primarily on gangs from the Midwest and the South. These include African American, Hispanic, Southeast Asian, and Caucasian gangs, as well as female gangs, Skinheads, and Taggers. Be aware, however, that there are as many gangs operating today as there are minorities: Filipino, Chinese, Native American, Korean, and Pacific Islander gangs, to name a few. Each has its own history, style of dress, customs, crime patterns, and affiliations. It is the reader's responsibility to ask local law enforcement officials about which gangs are operating in their area.

With that said, the following is a brief overview of the sections of this book:

• **The evolution of street gangs.** Gangs are not a new phenomenon. They have been around since the founding of this country. This is the smallest section of the book, and rightly so. There are a number of fine books available that go into great detail about the history of gangs. *This brief overview simply compares today's gangs with gangs throughout America's history.* It also provides a breakdown of specific gang nations, as well as their histories, philosophies, factions, and affiliations. For example, there are different factions within the numerous African American and Hispanic gangs across the nation. Some are at war with each other. Some have formed alliances. Each nation is discussed in detail so readers can focus on those affiliations that might apply to their geographic location. For specific neighborhood gang groups and affiliations, readers should contact their local police or probation department.

• **The lure of the gang.** Although gangs appear to be loosely knit (and in many cases do lack organization), large gangs are tightly structured and adhere to strict rules and bylaws. *This section covers the recruitment processes, organizational structures, hierarchical systems, and age and race demographics that vary from one gang to another.* It explains why gangs appeal to kids, and discusses actions members can take when they are ready to quit the gang lifestyle.

• **Children and gang behavior.** *This section explains how to use gang identifiers to determine if a child is involved with a gang.* An identifier can be clothing, jewelry, a word, a handwritten symbol, a certain color combination—anything a young person displays that might indicate gang involvement. One word of caution: If a child displays an identifier, he or she is not necessarily involved with a gang. Parents and educators should look for three or more identifiers before coming to a conclusion. Numbers count here. The more identifiers a child exhibits, the more likely it is that he or she is involved in gang activity.

- **Steering kids away from gangs.** *Section four discusses how communities, schools, and individuals can respond to the gang problem, and it suggests where to look for outside help.* This book cannot answer all of your questions; however, parents, school administrators, law enforcement personnel, and community leaders should be able to draw some useful ideas from these chapters and take a direct and decisive approach to the gang crisis.

This last section may prove to be the most controversial. Parents may find some unconventional methods here for dealing with their children and gangs. This is not the time for timidity. As gangs become bolder, parents must become bolder. If one method doesn't work, try another. You might also be uncomfortable with what is said about your own ideas and lifestyle. That's okay. The bottom line is, if you didn't care about what happens to your child, you would not have picked this book up in the first place, right?

Finally, don't give up. No matter what happens, try to leave a crack in the door. Even the most wayward, hard-headed kids need a glimmer of hope. When their methods have failed and they're ready to stop their gang activity, they may be ready to do things your way.

Strap in and hang on, reader. The road ahead might be bumpy, mind numbing, and frustrating, but we'll try to get through. We have to try.

Part One

The Evolution of Street Gangs

A Brief Overview

Chapter 1

AMERICAN GANGS SINCE 1826

Our proud nation has had a disturbingly long history of gangs. Gang-like activity was imported when European settlers made their way to America. As the young immigrant men rebelled against their low social and economic status, gangs began to evolve.

THE 1800S TO THE 1920S

The first known organized gang was formed in the back of a small grocery store in the Five Points District of New York City. The year was 1826, and Edward Coleman had gathered together some of New York's finest pickpockets and thieves to form the Forty Thieves gang. Thereafter, citizens and law enforcement officials were fearful to venture into the gang's territory. The second gang to form (ironically, in the same grocery store where the Forty Thieves were formed) was the Kerryonians. Their name derived from County Kerry, Ireland. Within a few years, other organized gangs formed in the back rooms of grocery stores. Among them were the Chichesten, Roach Guards, Plug Uglies, Shirt Tails, and Dead Rabbits.[1]

Not far from the Five Points District, gangs were beginning to organize in the area known as the Bowery. The largest of these gangs was the Bowery Boys, but other gangs were starting to make names for themselves as well: the Atlantic Guards, O'Connell Guards, True Blue American Guards, and American Guards. The Bowery gangs' chief activity was street brawling with the Five Point gangs. They fought over territory just as gangs fight over turf today.[2]

Like today's gangs, the gangs of yesteryear wore distinctive clothing to identify themselves. According to James Haskins, author of *Street Gangs: Yesterday and Today,* the Plug Uglies were named for their large plug hats, which they stuffed with wool and leather to serve as protective helmets in battle. Similarly, the Shirt Tails distinguished themselves by defying accepted fashions and wearing their shirts outside their trousers. The Roach Guards wore a blue stripe on their pantaloons (trousers), the Dead Rabbits a red stripe. Of all the Bowery gangs, the True Blue Americans wore the most distinctive uniforms: stove pipe hats and ankle-length frock coats.[3]

The 1920s

As the population of the eastern United States headed west, so did the gangs. By the post–Civil War period, more than fifty years after the formation of the first organized gang, there were thousands of gangs divided primarily along ethnic, racial, and cultural lines. In 1927, Frederick M. Thrasher, a noted criminologist, studied more than 1,300 Chicago gangs. A little more than 7 percent were African American gangs; the rest were mainly of European descent. At that time, Irish, Italian, German, and Polish immigrants were moving into various communities in and around Chicago. Many of these gangs evolved into major crime syndicates during and after Prohibition. In large cities throughout the United States, these syndicates fought gang wars for control of specific territories and illegal activities like bookmaking, extortion, gun running, and liquor sales.

The 1930s and the 1940s

Though gangs of European descent still outnumbered all others during the 1930s and 1940s, the trend was beginning to change. More African Americans, Puerto Ricans, and Mexican Americans moved into the northern cities during this period. As the citizens of these neighborhoods began to change, the roots of today's gangs started to evolve.

Mexican American gang members, at that time, were called "pachucos" and dressed in zoot suits. The zoot suit consisted of tapered pants worn high on the waist; long, wide-shouldered coats; and large-brimmed hats. Gang members as well as law-abiding young men wore the zoot suit as a fashion statement. This style of dress would later become a symbol of youth defiance in Los Angeles, when police arrested everyone wearing zoot suits, whether or not they were gang members. Visiting soldiers and white citizens, too, would harass anyone who wore a zoot suit. This harassment led to racial conflict, arrests, and ultimately, murder. In 1943, a gang of zoot suiters attacked eleven sailors in downtown Los Angeles. In retaliation, hundreds of sailors came into the neighborhood over the next few nights and proceeded to beat the local pachucos. The skirmishes gathered momentum until one night, several thousand servicemen and civilians marched into downtown Los Angeles and attacked anyone dressed as a pachuco. Law enforcement personnel looked the other way, arresting the beaten pachucos while ignoring the servicemen who were doing the assaulting. This event was later referred to as the zoot-suit riots.

The 1950s and the 1960s

Between 1941 and 1956, over 500,000 Puerto Ricans immigrated to the United States, with a large percentage settling in New York City. Hispanic gangs grew rapidly after World War II as European immigrants left their neighborhoods and Puerto Ricans became the new tenants.

In the 1950s, the level of gang warfare between African American and Hispanic gangs reached an all-time high in cities like Chicago, New York, Detroit, Boston, Philadelphia, and Los Angeles. Fighting occurred for any number of reasons—racial differences, turf disputes, even the defense of a woman's honor. Gangs fought with knives, bats, chains, and homemade weapons, or simply their own hands. Occasionally, they turned automobile radio antennas into homemade guns (called zip guns) if regular guns were unavailable. Gangs referred to fighting as "jiggerbugging," "bopping," or "rumbling," depending on which area of the country they lived in. Alcohol, heroin, and marijuana became a common part of gang culture.

Gang members at that time wore handmade sweaters, showing their gang colors and insignia, and black leather jackets with metal studs, with the wearer's name and name of the gang stitched on the back. For example, Maus Maus, a Hispanic gang from New York City named after a tribe of fierce warriors from Africa, wore black leather jackets with two red Ms stitched on the back. Jackets and sweaters were prized as ultimate status symbols, and gang members would die before giving them up to a rival gang. Conversely, gang members coveted rival gang members' sweaters and jackets and would use violence as a means to procure them.

During the 1960s, when national attention turned to civil rights, the Vietnam War, and riots in urban areas, new groups with political agendas emerged and gang membership began to decline. In 1966, the Black Panthers formed in Oakland, California, quickly gaining national prominence. The Black Muslim movement also gained significant ground with its recruitment.

THE 1970S

Political unrest in the seventies prompted the immigration of over one million Asian refugees to the United States. The language and socioeconomic barriers they faced resulted in the formation of Southeast Asian gangs. As the Vietnam War drew to a close and urban ghetto riots became smoldering memories, African American, Hispanic, and Caucasian gangs began to reassemble and proliferate once again. Music, television, and movies began a trend toward greater violence, and the new gangs reflected this change. They now had access to more powerful weapons, and they were not afraid to use them. Conflicts became more violent. Older members had younger members perform violent crimes to avoid lengthy jail or prison sentences. Black leather jackets gave way to sports team Starter jackets, and other identifiers began to evolve—hand signals and graffiti walls, for example—which gangs continue to use today. The Crips and Bloods formed, and several gangs began their movement toward national status.

Chapter 2

AFRICAN AMERICAN, HISPANIC, SOUTHEAST ASIAN, AND CAUCASIAN GANGS

African American Gangs

African American gangs of the 1990s are beginning to follow a pattern that is characteristic of Hispanic gangs: a generation cycle. Children are being raised in homes where one or both parents belong to a gang. As a result, the gang atmosphere permeates the children's upbringing. More and more children are being raised by teenage mothers and fathers who refuse—or are unable—to let go of gang life.

There are four main groups of African American gangs in the United States: the Crips, Bloods, Folks, and People. The Crips and Bloods can be found mostly in California and other western states, but there are a number of them throughout the entire country. Both Hispanic and African American gangs in the eastern, southern, and midwestern states tend to maintain alliances with two main nations, the Folk and the People. Each of these four groups has its own unique history.

Crips

There are several stories about how one of the largest gangs, the Crips, earned its name. Each story sounds plausible, but the legends have been passed through so many individuals that the actual truth may never be known.

In the 1991 national bestseller *Do or Die,* author Leòn Bing writes about life among the Crips and the Bloods. During an interview with Jim Galipeau of the Los Angeles County Probation Department, Bing learns one story of the origin of the name "Crips":

> Then in 1968, 1969, somewhere in there, a kid named Raymond Washington pulled together a little gang of kids at Fremont High School in Watts. As it happened, a large percentage of neighborhood residents in the Watts area were Japanese, many of them older, sixty and up. The night arrived when a bunch of these older folks went to a block club meeting, and after it was adjourned, they decided to go for coffee before they walked over to catch the bus on Central Avenue. As they were toddling along toward the corner, here comes Raymond and a bunch of his homeboys, bearing down on them like a pack of wild dogs. The old people did what the cops had told them to do: they yelled, they screamed, they carried on. And sure enough, two things happened: the kids, scared off by all the commotion, ran away after grabbing only a couple of purses, and the police arrived on the scene very quickly. Things became a bit funny, because to these older Asian Americans, all people looked the same. Except for one lady. She kept repeating over and over that one of the kids was 'a crip. A crip with a stick.' The cops were finally able to make out, through this torrent of

> fractured English, that what the lady was trying to tell them was that one of the boys who attacked them had a game leg and that he was carrying a cane. A cripple with a stick. Whatever police reporter was hanging around the station that night picked up that word, crip, and bam, Raymond's little gang of thugs had a name.[4]

Another story claims this same individual, Raymond Washington, named the gang after the comic book *Tales from the Crypt*. Yet another story holds that the Crips were named after the largest gang in South Central Los Angeles, the Cribs. Whichever version is true, today, Crips are the arch enemies of the Bloods. Many bloody feuds have been fought between these two groups. It is also interesting to note that because the number of Crips has reached unwieldy proportions, there has been much in-fighting, Crip against Crip.

The Crips adopted the color blue because of the blue bandannas members purchased to conceal their faces while committing crimes. The bandanna, when not in use, hangs from a back pocket. As a sign of pride, members wear other articles of blue clothing, as well.

Bloods

The Bloods' name also has a number of possible origins. Some authorities believe the name comes from the gang color, red, although others have said the use of the color red comes from their gang name, Bloods. Another possible explanation is that during the 1960s, only two colors of bandannas were available in stores, and the Crips had already staked a claim on blue. It has also been suggested that the Pirus, the original Blood members, adopted the color well before the Bloods formed.

Bloods and Crips originated in the late 1960s in the cities of Compton and Watts, and in the Willowbrook area of Southeast Los Angeles. The young men who lived on and near Piru Street, which passes through this particular geographical area, were tired of being pressured by Crip members to join. So they formed their own gang. This immediately set the two gangs apart as sworn enemies. The new gang's members referred to themselves as the Compton Piru gang. As gang membership increased, the Compton Pirus splintered into many different factions—West Side Pirus, Avenue Pirus, Neighborhood Pirus, Senter Park Pirus, B-Bop Watts, Outlaw Twenties, and Six-Deuce Brims, to name a few. In time, gangs such as the Bounty Hunters, Brims, and Denver Lanes also spread throughout Los Angeles County. These gangs sprang out of the Piru gangs; however, they were far enough beyond the Piru Street area to refer to themselves by a different name—Bloods. Today, many Piru gangs outside of the southeastern part of Los Angeles identify themselves as Bloods, and the terms Piru and Blood are synonymous.

Because the Crips far outnumber the Bloods, there is, out of necessity, less fighting between Blood gangs. It should also be noted that Bloods, for whatever reason, are more ruthless and violent when dealing with rival gangs.

Folk and People Nations

Many smaller gangs are affiliated with one of the large *gang nations,* which are predominantly, but not exclusively, African American. During the 1960s and 1970s, incarcerated gang members built coalitions, bringing smaller gangs together to protect themselves against larger ones. As these coalitions developed, alliances were formalized through actual written treaties establishing rules, bylaws, and so forth, much the same way national or international treaties are formed by heads of state.

Although consisting primarily of African American gangs, the Folk and People Nations comprise numerous white and Hispanic gangs as well. Presented here is a general overview of only the larger gangs within these gang nations. It should be further noted that in some regions, the Crips and the Bloods (who have worked their way east and southeast from California and other western states), have formed alliances with the Folk and People Nations to help ensure strength in numbers. In these regions, the Crips ally themselves with the Folks, and the Bloods with the People. Be sure to check with local law enforcement officials to determine the gang alliances in your region.

Black Gangster Disciples Nation (alliance: Folk Nation)
The Black Gangster Disciples Nation, also known by the initials BGD, is rooted in Chicago. Its membership in Chicago and other midwestern states numbers over 25,000. The gang was originally called the Devil's Disciples (named after original gang members found a pair of jeans with the logo of a devil and pitchfork on it and adopted this logo as their own). The name was later changed to the Black Gangster Disciples. This gang was formed in the early 1960s by a drug dealer named David Barksdale, who was assassinated in 1974. After his death, several smaller groups split off from the Black Gangster Disciples, including the Gangster Disciples, Black Disciples, and the prison gang, Brothers of the Struggle (or BOS). Larry Hoover, organizer of the Gangster Disciples, was convicted of murder in 1973 and sentenced to 150 to 200 years in prison. Although he denies it, Hoover maintains control of the Gangster Disciples from his prison cell. The Black Disciples was formed by a man named Shorty Freeman. Both factions are involved in a very bloody feud over prime narcotics territory.

Vice Lord Nation (alliance: People Nation)

The Vice Lord Nation was started as a club in the 1950s by young men serving time at the Illinois State Training School for Boys in St. Charles, Illinois. After being released, a number of these young men relocated their gang to Chicago's West Side. About ten factions broke away from the main group and can still be found in various cities around the country. Each faction has its own name and leader. One of the largest and most organized factions was called the Unknown Conservative Vice Lords. In 1985, it obtained a charter from the state of Illinois as a nonprofit voters group called the United Concerned Voters League. Identical initials were no accident. The gang was awarded federal assistance, but the money was mismanaged to line the coffers of the gang leaders. The Unknown Conservative Vice Lords no longer exists; rather, it split into the Unknown Vice Lords and the Conservative Vice Lords.

Other factions operating within the Vice Lord Nation are the 4 Corner Hustlers, Undertaker Vice Lords, Gangster Stone Vice Lords, Insane Vice Lords, Imperial Insane Vice Lords, Mafia Insane Vice Lords, and Ebony Vice Lords.

Because of the death and imprisonment of many of its leaders, the Vice Lord Nation almost ceased to exist during the 1970s. A revival of the gang occurred in the early 1980s, when incarcerated gang members were released from prison and returned to Chicago. (For more information on the history of the Vice Lord Nation, see Appendix One at the back of this book.)

El Rukns (alliance: People Nation)

The El Rukns gang started out as the Blackstone Rangers in the early 1960s. When Jeff Fort assumed leadership in the late sixties, he changed the name to the Black P [Peace] Stone Nation. It wasn't until the early 1970s, when he became incarcerated, that the name was changed to El Rukns. Originally formed as a coalition of almost fifty gangs, it became the supreme power in Chicago's South Side.

Like the Unknown Conservative Vice Lords, the Black P Stone Nation members tried to legitimize their existence in the community by acting as social leaders. They, too, received a charter from the state of Illinois, calling themselves the Grassroots Independent Voters of Illinois. Although the gang received federal funding and private donations at first, misuse of the funds landed Jeff Fort in prison. Later, the El Rukns attempted to proclaim themselves a religious organization, but were defeated in court.

African American gangs are generally motivated by profit. Drug selling is their most valuable enterprise, and territory is everything. This is especially true if a particular street corner or property is a base for drug pushers. Gangs will guard their turf against rival gangs, whom they view as trying to take away their drug business. As a result of their drug enterprises, African American gangs are frequently involved with criminal activities such as weapons violations, extortion, assault, robbery, intimidation, drive-by shootings, and so forth. When it comes to the drug trade, these gangs can be unforgiving.

This point became clear to me some years back when I worked with a couple of juveniles who had joined up with a gang based in Chicago. They made the unfortunate blunder of selling look-alike drugs to some very intense individuals on the street. (Look-alike drugs, or "drywall," are false drugs—crushed Alka Seltzer and aspirin, for example, that are passed off as real drugs, or drugs that are so diluted with other substances they have no potency.) Little did they know, the individuals who bought the drugs were in a rival gang. To make matters worse, they sold the look-alike drugs in the rival gang's territory. A contract was placed on them, and several days later, a hit squad from Chicago was dispatched to Waukegan.

The young men were ambushed. One was killed instantly in a hail of gunfire; the other was laid out with two shots. As if to make an example of the boys, a member of the hit squad fired four more shots into the second boy's back.

Miraculously, the second young man survived, although he is now paralyzed and confined to a wheelchair. You would think the incident would have ended his attraction to the gang lifestyle. No way. Six months later he was sent to prison, wheelchair and all, for selling drugs to an undercover agent. I saw this young man again several years later while making a home visit in a gang-infested neighborhood. He was sitting in his wheelchair, surrounded by gang brothers, swigging down beer. Having been paroled only three weeks before, he was already back with his gang. He remembered me from the days when I worked with him as his probation officer, before he and his friend were ambushed. I talked with him for a time, ignoring the stares from the other gang members. His stance and loyalty to the gang was unwavering, a kind of "live by the sword, die by the sword" mentality. He did say, however, that he had given up selling look-alike drugs.

The point of this story is to inform. African American gangs have very definite territorial boundaries within their neighborhoods, and they will not tolerate rival gangs selling drugs—especially look-alike drugs—on their turf.

Hispanic Gangs

The first Hispanic gangs developed in the early 1900s as small, loosely-knit neighborhood groups. Formed during the late 1930s and early 1940s, Hispanic gangs organized to protect themselves from outside influences, such as neighborhood criminals and unwelcome government or law enforcement officials.

The most prominent features of Hispanic gangs are their devout loyalty to the neighborhood, or turf, and their single-minded devotion to the gang and its members. Kinship within Hispanic gangs has a long tradition. It is not unusual for fathers, sons, and uncles to all belong to the same gang. When third and fourth generations of a family belong to a gang, breaking the cycle is extremely difficult, if not impossible. The gang member sees his or her family in the gang and would not think twice about laying down his or her life for the cause.

This sense of family unity within the Hispanic gang structure has been frustrating for law enforcement personnel. Rarely does a Hispanic gang member go to law enforcement officials to inform on another gang member. Not only would this be looked upon by fellow gang members with disdain, at times it would cause the informant's own family to be placed in peril. Retribution is common among Hispanic gangs. In fact, many Hispanic gang members will not cooperate with a police investigation or testify in court if one of their own members has been hurt or killed by a rival gang. Rather, they punish the rival gang in their own manner.

Hispanic gang members will not just "hang out" with each other as other gang members do, but will immerse themselves totally in whatever gang activity is taking place at the moment. Such complete involvement earns the title "cholo," or "the dude." To obtain this title, the most feared, crazy, and respected gang member will act out on the public—and even on his or her fellow gang members—in explosive ways. Once a gang member has earned that title, he or she will sometimes tattoo three dots on the back of his or her hand. Three dots represent "Mi Vida Loca," which translates to "my crazy life."

Latin Kings (alliance: People Nation)

The largest known Hispanic gang, the Latin Kings, is not exclusively Hispanic; whites and African Americans are also members.

Founded in the early 1960s in South Chicago and the Humboldt Park area on the northwest side of Chicago, the Latin Kings and their factions have spread throughout the United States. Latin Kings are extremely organized and have been known to hold national meetings.

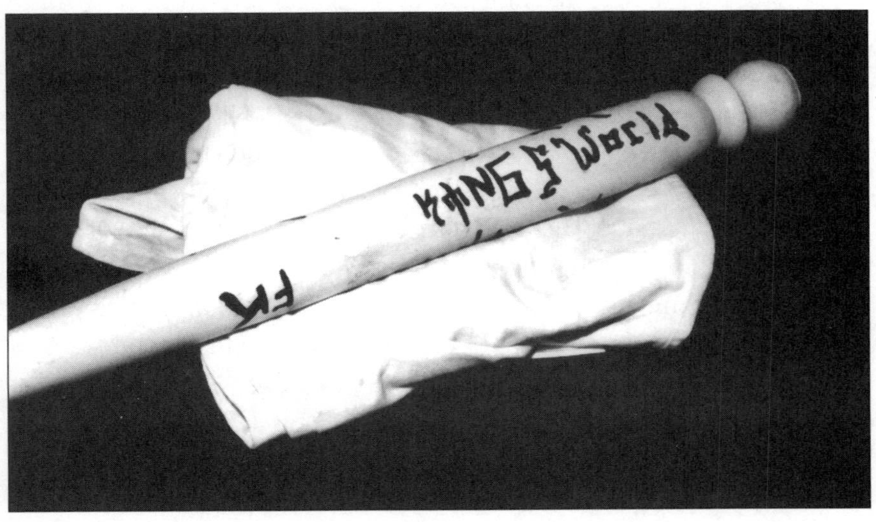

This weapon, fashioned from a bedpost, was confiscated from a member of the Latin Kings.

Maniac Latin Disciples (alliance: Folk Nation)

The Maniac Latin Disciples gang, which also goes by the name Latin Disciples, was founded in Chicago in the late sixties by an individual with the street name Hitler. Because Hitler was killed by the Latin Kings in 1970, much of the gang's graffiti contains a backward swastika in memory of their leader. The swastika is placed backward to distinguish it from the Skinhead or neo-Nazi swastika. As in the Latin Kings, membership is not restricted to Hispanics. Whites and African Americans belong as well.

Because the Latin Kings and Maniac Latin Disciples are aligned with different nations—the People and Folk—they are automatic enemies. Both gangs expanded in the 1970s when smaller gangs, whose size left them at a disadvantage when dealing with rival gangs, began to merge with them. This was especially true during the 1980s when crack cocaine became the hot-selling drug. Hispanic gangs were quick to find out that drug money equaled power, and power meant further expansion—into the suburbs as well as other states.

18th Street (alliance: none)

The largest known Hispanic gang originating in southern California is the 18th Street gang. This gang is twenty times larger than a typical area gang and, with over 20,000 members in southern California alone, is much larger than the better known Bloods and Crips.

The 18th Street gang gained its initial foothold in Los Angeles during the 1960s, and has expanded at an astonishing rate. In Los Angeles alone, the gang is so large that it has been divided into five different groups according to region: 18th Street, 18th Street Eastside, 18th Street Northside, 18th Street Southside, and 18th Street Westside. But the 18th Street gang has not confined its activities to California. Law enforcement officials in Oregon report that the 18th Street gang is the largest and fastest growing gang in their state. It has also spread to Utah, Arizona, Missouri, New Mexico, Texas, and

Washington, and has even been found in El Salvador and Honduras. One reason for this rapid expansion is the gang's involvement with illicit drugs. The 18th Street gang is reportedly large enough and powerful enough to receive its drugs directly from the Colombian and Mexican cartels.

Unlike the African American gangs, which are controlled by one or several individuals, the 18th Street gang has no national leader. Rather, it is controlled by older gang members who oversee daily operations.

	Folk Nation	**People Nation**	**No Affiliation**
African American Gangs	Black Gangster Disciples	Vice Lords; El Rukns	
Hispanic Gangs	Maniac Latin Disciples	Latin Kings	18th Street

Southeast Asian Gangs

During the 1970s, political unrest prompted the immigration of over one million Asian refugees to the United States. Among the largest groups to find refuge in this country were Vietnamese, Filipinos, Laotians, Hmong, and Cambodians. Like the Europeans who came to the United States in the early nineteenth century, Southeast Asians faced substantial language and socioeconomic barriers, which led to the formation of gangs.

Initially, Southeast Asian gangs feuded among themselves, but this has become less common over the years. Although many

Southeast Asian gangs have adopted the dress and graffiti of African American and Hispanic gangs, they tend to place less emphasis on such trappings. What makes these gangs unique is where they commit their crimes, and which weapons they use to carry out their crimes.

Southeast Asian gangs are motivated by money, and they primarily burglarize businesses and residences for revenue. They do not, however, adhere to any hard-and-fast rules when it comes to turf. The entire city and surrounding areas are theirs; they recognize no boundaries. Some Southeast Asian gangs, called Traveling Gangs, travel across state lines to commit their crimes. Members of these gangs have contacts, which might have been established during time spent in immigrant relocation camps, in many cities across the country. Traveling Gangs do not adopt group names, but they do have a hierarchical structure. Individual assignments are given by the gang leader before each burglary or robbery. Gang members generally travel to specific businesses and homes with prior knowledge of the valuables to be found on the property. Sometimes the location will even be photographed in advance.

Some Southeast Asian gangs do not travel; neither do they follow directives from any one person. These gangs are classified as Informal Gangs. Their criminal activity frequently involves burglary, car theft, and extortion, and is usually confined to a specific territory..

Southeast Asian gangs parlay the rewards of their successful crime ventures—cold, hard cash—into weapons. But not just any weapons. Automatic assault rifles and semiautomatic handguns are now the weapons of choice among Southeast Asian gangs, much more so than the lowly Saturday night specials. Sawed-off shotguns and butterfly knives are still sometimes used because they are so easy to conceal. Parents will rarely see any of these weapons in their own home, however. Older gang members will often rent a residential home, called a safe house, to store their weapons and stolen loot.

Southeast Asian gangs follow the tradition of Hispanic gangs in that family members, relatives, and neighbors tend to belong to the same gang. But again, there are no hard-and-fast rules here. It is not unheard of for family members to belong to different gangs. If they happen to live under the same roof, there is inevitably a great amount of tension within the family.

Caucasian Gangs

Society generally tends to believe that gang members are people of color. In truth, there are a large number of gangs made up almost exclusively of Caucasians. These gangs are not affiliated with Skinheads or Taggers (discussed in Chapter 3), nor are they affiliated with minority gangs. They do, however, adopt the same colors, symbols, sports team logos, styles of dress, hand signs, and slang as African American and Hispanic gangs, and emulate the same crime patterns, including drug distribution and drive-by shootings. For the most part, they will not adopt names that might associate them with the Crips, Lords, Disciples, Bloods, and so forth. Rather, they tend to choose names ending with words like Boys, Posse, Gangsters, or Crew.

Caucasian gangs began to form in the late 1980s, as individuals sought protection from other gangs at school or in their neighborhood. Like minority gangs, Caucasian gangs are growing rapidly. Members generally come from middle and upper-middle class families, and gang membership tends to range anywhere from twenty to one hundred. It is uncommon to find older adults acting as leaders, as they often do in minority gangs.

All of the identifiers discussed in this book may also be applied to white gangs.

Chapter 3

MISCELLANEOUS GANGS

FEMALE GANGS

Females have been a part of male gangs since the very beginning. Prior to the 1950s, females tended to be girlfriends of male gang members and rarely sought out or participated in hard-core gang activity. They were used by their male counterparts primarily for incidental purposes. If two gangs were about to fight, for example, the females carried the weapons, since male police officers wouldn't usually frisk females. Today, female gang members are sometimes used to transport drugs for the same reason. This practice is diminishing, however, as more and more women join the police force.

The last four decades have seen the emergence of female gangs, although usually as auxiliaries to male gangs. Since the female gang is an offshoot of the male gang, it is customary for each group to back each other up. Rarely does a female gang operate independently, or go "solo," and it is still not unusual for male gangs to use female members as decoys for rival male gang members.

Female gangs are usually not as demonstrative as male gangs and tend to be more reserved about their lifestyle and mannerisms. This is not to say they are less dangerous. There has been an alarming increase in the amount and severity of violence exhibited by female gangs recently. Also, in the last few years, more females have become involved with gang activity at a younger age, and parents of girls ages eleven and older should particularly take note. Experts say that 10 to 15 percent of all gangs are female, which means that there are tens of thousands of female gang members throughout the United States.

Skinhead Gangs

Skinhead gangs got their foothold in America during the mid-1980s, but their history can be traced back to England in the 1960s. In many small towns in Great Britain at that time, high unemployment along with a growing influx of immigrants from developing countries caused youths to become fearful. They feared they were being edged out of the job market, and saw the immigrants as a threat to the white working class. This fear grew into the intense hatred and extreme nationalism that pervade Skinhead gangs today. The hatred of the new immigrants spilled over to include Jews and other minorities as well.

The Skinheads' manner and style of dress was formulated at that time to reflect their working-class roots. The term "skinhead" refers to the practice of gang members shaving their heads, which they did to avoid having their hair pulled during physical confrontations with police or pedestrians.

The music of the sixties also played a part in the growth and identification of the Skinhead movement. Skinhead music—yes, there are specific music groups just for Skinheads—gradually became known as "Oi" (pronounced like the "oi" in "oil" and meaning "us versus them"). Skinheads use this word in Europe and the United States as a universal greeting to one another.

Today's Skinheads come from all income levels; they may be male or female. They frequently have academic problems, use excessive amounts of drugs or alcohol, and many are victims of physical or sexual abuse. Skinheads hate all types of authority. They tend to be "loners," often feeling alienated from family, society, and the government. Alienated individuals are at a greater risk of being recruited into the Skinhead movement, because they hope to gain superiority and power through intimidation.

Over the last two decades, the American Skinhead movement has established ties with more traditional white supremacy groups, such as the Ku Klux Klan and the Aryan Nation. Along with these alliances comes a more extreme ideology, as well as a more intense hatred and prejudice toward minorities, gays, and Jews.

The Skinheads themselves are splintered into two different factions: the Racists and the Antiracists. Racists, the most narrowly-focused individuals, are made up of three different subgroups: White Power, White Pride, and White Supremacy. The White Supremacy gang, over the years, has been given the names Boot Boys, Hammer Skins, Nazi Skins, LADS (L.A. Death Squad), The Northern Hammerskins, the WAY, the ORDER, and Hitler Youth. The difference between the three subgroups lies in the intensity and commitment each displays. They are the hard-core members. Their philosophy states that all people of color are inferior, and that race mixing and homosexuality are abominations to God and country and should be stopped by any means necessary. They also believe that Jews control all financial institutions, media, and governments worldwide.

While African American, Hispanic, and Southeast Asian gangs are motivated by money, the goal of Racist Skinheads is to spread hate. They do this through public demonstrations, literature, and graffiti. Racists view themselves as the white working class and claim that it was their white fathers and forefathers who built this nation. The achievements and contributions of other groups are considered insignificant and often looked upon with disdain.

As Racist Skinheads started to emerge in this country, the second, smaller group of Skinheads, the Antiracist Skinheads, began to evolve. Antiracists have a multiracial membership, but adhere to the same style of dress, haircut, and preference in music as the Racists. The Antiracist view, however, is that everyone is equal and should not be discriminated against because of skin color, religion, or heritage. This difference has resulted in many bloody brawls between the Antiracists and Racists. Antiracist gangs have a variety of names, each promoting the idea of racial harmony: Mud Skins, Two-Tone Skins, and Racial Unity Skinheads. The most widely known Antiracist gang is Skinheads Against Racial Prejudice, or SHARP. In the eighties, SHARP had a reputation of being more prone to violence than other gangs, and many Antiracist Skinheads disassociated themselves from the group.

TAGGER GANGS

Tagger gangs, sometimes called crews, cliques, or posses, have been around for a number of years. Taggers are graffiti artists; the city is their canvas. Tagger gangs are generally made up of teens who use spray paint, felt pens, and paint brushes. Their artwork—which police and city officials call vandalism—can be found on buildings and city walls, in subways and parking garages, on water towers, on train station platforms, and on the sides of trains. Trains are especially prized by Taggers; their artwork rolls out from the train station early in the morning to thousands of ready-made art patrons (daily commuters). Railroad personnel scramble to keep up with Taggers, covering the artwork with heavy solvents.

Taggers will spend days putting their ideas down on paper, making rough sketches and assigning colors to patterns. Then, under the cover of night, Taggers will spend eight to ten hours painting the side of a train. Their artwork can be intricate, colorful, and complex. Their names will usually accompany the graffiti. All that work for a week's worth of glory, at most.

While traditional gangs are often amazed by Taggers' artwork, there are times when conflicts arise. Because Taggers create their artwork wherever they feel like it, turf boundaries are sometimes violated. Traditional gangs have been known to retaliate against Tagger gangs, which has led some Taggers to join other traditional gangs for protection. There are also incidents where one Tagger gang has intentionally painted over another's artwork, leading to violence as Tagger gangs attempt to claim territory. Some Taggers now carry weapons to their painting sites.

Taggers are proud of their artwork. They take photographs of their graffiti, knowing that their work will be short-lived. Taggers often place these photographs in an album, much the same way a new mother puts photos of her newborn child in a family scrapbook. They keep these graffiti "portfolios" as trophies to show to other Taggers. Some years back, there was a television movie about a graffiti Tagger. Despite the usual plot relating violent confrontations and a breakdown of family dynamics, this story had an unusual ending. A caring social worker, seeing the potential in this misguided Tagger, had him show his photo album to a corporate executive, who hired the young teenager as a beginning graphic artist.

A reality check, if you please. Taggers, for the most part, write their graffiti for the sheer excitement of it, and for their own gratification. As a bridge to future employment? I don't think so. Graffiti costs American taxpayers untold millions of dollars each year, and most businesses are unforgiving of such vandalism.

Part Two

The Lure of the Gang

Why Kids Join, How They Can Leave

Chapter 4

WHAT IS A STREET GANG?

Simply put, a street gang is a cohesive group of three or more individuals, generally between the ages of eleven and twenty-five, who usually claim a neighborhood or geographical territory. Street gangs have a definite structure with some form of leadership, and members wear distinctive clothing, use special street names, languages, symbols, and signs, and commit organized and spontaneous criminal acts collectively or individually within the community.

Definitions among police throughout the United States are similar, but vary from region to region. To some, a gang may comprise four or five older individuals in their thirties or forties who gather, drink beer, and go out and commit crimes. No special clothing, signs, or symbols are used. No drive-by shootings are committed. To others, a gang might be a loosely-knit group of suburban high-schools kids who gather, get high, and go out and vandalize property. Here, too, there may be no other gang identifiers. The term "gang" may ultimately be used by local police departments and news media to describe everyday troublemakers. As a result, the public at large has a distorted view of the so-called gang problem. But make no mistake, the gangs discussed in this book are large, well established, ruthless, and firmly entrenched.

In the 1960s, there were approximately eighty-five cities nationwide that reported gangs or gang activity. Over a thousand cities now report gang activity. To deny that gang migration is increasing would be absurd.

A 1996 study by the National Youth Gang Center reports that there are more than 600,000 gang members in the United States, and over 25,000 gangs. Because this study did not take rural communities into account, however, the numbers are likely to be much higher. Furthermore, because suburban communities frequently underreport gang statistics by at least 50 percent, the National Youth Gang Center estimates that the actual number of gang members operating in the United States may be between 850,00, and 900,000.

While we're on the subject, the term "street gang" should be separated from "youth gang." "Youth gang" was popular some years ago (some of the older generation still use the phrase) and should, in my opinion, be retired. The title "street gang" may seem a bit derogatory to some, but it seems to fit the situation nicely. Because street gangs are made up of both juveniles and adults, the title "youth gang" doesn't really apply anymore.

Ages of Gang Members

It has been reported in recent years that more young kids are becoming involved with gangs and gang activity. This may be true to some degree. The fact is, however, that young children living in gang-infested neighborhoods have always been exposed to gang activity. It only becomes news when a very young child kills or is killed.

Whether young kids are recruited or join on their own, whether the recruitment of children has always been the case or is a recent phenomenon, one thing is certain: kids become involved with gangs at surprisingly young ages. The following are the average age groups of kids belonging to different types of gangs. Be forewarned, however, that these are only generalizations. There are no hard-and-fast rules with regard to age.

African American Gangs

Until recently, the typical African American gang member was between the ages of twelve and twenty-five. Today, children between the ages of eight and eleven have become more involved with gangs and gang activity. It is still the exception, however. At least for now. That young children are becoming involved in gangs really hit home in 1994, when a juvenile male named Robert Sandifer (street name "Yummy") made front-page news in Chicago and around the country.

Robert had been involved in a drive-by shooting of rival gang members, and had shot and killed an innocent fourteen-year-old girl in the process. A member of the Black Disciples for almost a year, he had been arrested two years earlier for armed robbery and had a lengthy felony rap sheet. Three days after Robert killed the girl, members of his own gang shot and killed him for bringing too much police attention to the gang. Robert was eleven years old.

Because of his age, the incident made national news headlines and became the focus of numerous articles on gang violence. Most eleven-year-olds don't go out and gun people down, of course. This case does point out, however, that younger children are being influenced by gangs and gang activity. Gang members who start in their preteens and survive into their twenties without being killed or incarcerated can count themselves extremely lucky.

Hard-core African American gang members are usually in their mid-teens to mid-twenties, although members in their thirties or forties can usually be found within the prison system. An emerging trend shows individuals in their twenties joining gangs for the first time. The draw is obvious: there is a lot of money to be made in the primary African American gang trade—drugs. Lack of employment opportunities, particularly in the poorer sections of town, may be a factor contributing to this alarming trend.

Hispanic Gangs

The typical age of the Hispanic gang member ranges from ten to twenty-three. Because the gang lifestyle is often passed down from generation to generation, kids are introduced to the gang at an early age. Older members occasionally settle down, finding new responsibilities in starting a family or a job. Although they may no longer be involved in gang-related activities, many former gang members maintain contact with both former and active members. Older ex-gang members are sometimes viewed by younger members as elder statesmen.

Southeast Asian Gangs

Generally speaking, very few Asian youngsters under the age of twelve get involved with gangs. Most Southeast Asian gang members are between sixteen and twenty-five years old. There are, however, formally organized Southeast Asian criminal groups with national and international ties, most notably to larger, more organized Chinese criminal groups like the United Bamboo and Wah Ching. Many Southeast Asian gang members "graduate" to these syndicates once they reach their twenties.

Caucasian Gangs

The age of the typical Caucasian gang member ranges from twelve to twenty-two, although members are primarily of junior high and high school age. Caucasian gangs are a relatively new phenomenon; they don't have strong roots like Hispanic and African American gangs do. Leaders tend to be individuals in their late teens or early twenties and are generally experts at some aspect of gang activity, such as fighting or using weapons.

Female Gangs

Female gang members are usually younger than their male counterparts. Their ages range from eleven to eighteen years old. The younger females, eleven to twelve years old, usually associate with older members, but do not often participate in violent crimes. They tend to commit crimes like shoplifting, truancy, and so on, whereas older female gang members are generally involved with the same types of crimes that male gang members perpetrate. It is not unheard of for older female gang members to participate in assaults, robberies, and drive-by shootings. Violence between female gang members can be just as intense and deadly as it is between male gang members.

Skinhead Gangs

Skinhead gangs have a more definitive age bracket, ranging from twelve to twenty-five years old. Rarely does anyone see a Skinhead in elementary school. But a word of caution is in order here: even if elementary school children do not dress the part, the Skinhead philosophy and ideology may still be present. Many parents who are involved with the KKK or other white supremacy groups are more than happy to pass along their prejudices and racism to their offspring. Parents and educators should watch children closely for any derogatory comments toward African Americans, Jews, or other minorities. The same holds true for anything written on school notebooks, whether in words or symbols.

As in Southeast Asian gangs, older Skinheads sometimes move up to larger, more organized white supremacy groups. This lessens their contact with law enforcement while allowing them to maintain their basic racist philosophy.

Tagger Gangs

Tagger gang members usually range from twelve years old to early twenties. Younger Taggers often act as lookouts for older Taggers and concentrate on tagging readily accessible areas like schools, phone booths, and street signs. Older Taggers target more difficult areas, such as trains, underpasses, and bridges.

Structure and Hierarchy

Like any organization, a street gang requires structure in order to operate efficiently. Though gangs tend to operate differently from region to region, there are similarities among the structures of each. Most gangs are made up of young males, and sometimes females, between the ages of eleven and twenty-five. The typical structure of a large street gang incorporates the following levels of hierarchy.

Group 1: Leaders

Older members—those with a more extensive criminal background, usually provide gang leadership. For example, the Gangster Disciples gang has between 18,000 and 25,000 members, yet for the most part, it is controlled by one man, Larry Hoover, who is serving out a 150 to 200 year sentence in prison. From his jail cell, Hoover delegates business to a number of area leaders within different communities. Most area leaders are in their twenties and have been in prison at least once.

Street gang leaders are ruthless in their leadership and expect other members to do their bidding without question. They must be logical, streetwise, mentally and physically tough, and able to become violent at a moment's notice.

Leadership in street gangs can be transitory. A leader may be challenged physically or politically at any time by another up-and-coming, hard-core member. If the incumbent leader loses, a new leader emerges. This rarely happens, however. A street gang leader has had to prove him or herself in the climb up the leadership ladder, usually through continued acts of extreme violence. Such acts of violence may cause another member to think twice before offering a challenge.

Leaders may also be toppled by the judicial process. Police and politicians steer investigations toward gang leaders, and when a leader is incarcerated or killed, a new leader emerges from the ranks of the hard-core membership. A good example occurred recently in Chicago, when a large number of Gangster Disciples leaders were indicted by the state attorney's office. A number of gang killings occurred in the ensuing days, as gang members jockeyed for leadership positions.

Group 2: Hard-core Members

Hard-core members are typically young adults in their late teens and early twenties. Many have had minimal schooling; high-school graduates are extremely rare. Their lives are completely immersed in the gang culture, even to the exclusion of their own biological families. To them, the gang is their family. Hard-core members plan and carry out gang activity under no other authority but the gang's. They initiate drug sales, buy weapons, go on drive-by shootings, and perform internal duties. These duties include collecting dues and teaching younger members the gang's constitution, rules, and by-laws.

Hard-core members, who make up 5 to 15 percent of gang membership, live by the rules of the gang and will lay down their life to defend them. They will kill anyone who dishonors the rules, including fellow members. If your son or daughter is already a hard-core member, he or she may be beyond the reach of intervention. There is more hope for the associate, or affiliate, gang member.

GROUP 3: ASSOCIATE GANG MEMBERS

Associate, or affiliate, members represent the second largest population segment of a gang—30 to 35 percent. Although they do not commit as much extreme violence as hard-core members, associates can be a real threat to the community. Associates dress like, act out as, and claim to be gang members. They have gone through the initiation process and may have learned the gang's manifesto, hand signs, and symbols, but they still maintain a relationship with their biological family. Associates are more approachable, and intervention will have a greater likelihood of success.

GROUP 4: FRINGE, MARGINAL, AND WANNA-BE MEMBERS

The average fringe member is between eleven and thirteen years old. While not officially gang members, fringes (also called marginals or wanna-bes) like to talk and dress like gang members, and even flash the gang signs. As a whole, fringes can constitute up to two-thirds of the entire gang. Though these individuals are not included in the deepest, innermost workings of the gang, they add to the overall community problem of criminal gang activity. The fringe is a testing ground, and it is as fringe members that most kids prove themselves to the hard-core gang members. This makes them especially dangerous. These kids can be tested for a long time before they are initiated into a specific gang.

Once testing is over, youths who are accepted are then "jumped" or "courted" into the gang. Gang members will beat a prospective member, or the prospect will buy his or her way in. When individuals decide to buy their way into a gang, the price may be so costly (it can be in the thousands) that it forces them to commit crimes to obtain the money. As a rite of initiation, a prospective member is sometimes forced to perform a criminal act, such as participate in the drive-by shooting of a rival gang member.

Like associate members, fringes are susceptible to intervention if they are approached early enough. Otherwise, these youths become so enmeshed in the gang lifestyle that it becomes acceptable to them, exciting, and even normal. The experts say that without intervention, wanna-bes will soon become "gonna-bes."

Group 5: Clueless Members

There is a fifth level of involvement in gangs. It is not a formal position within a gang, but a class of youths at risk. There is not much written about these kids. I call them "the clueless." These are the kids who learn about gangs from TV, movies, and magazines. They may know gang members and secretly admire them, thinking that the gang lifestyle is cool and exciting. The clueless see gangs as a new fad. They may experiment with gang-like dress and slang, and even flash gang signs to their friends in jest, but they know they're not gang members.

I have worked with a number of these kids over the years. They don't know how dangerous their activity can be. They may talk the talk, but when things get scary, they can't walk the walk. These kids could be joking around at school, talking tough and flashing gang signs to their friends and classmates, when they suddenly find themselves confronted by real gang members. Even joking around becomes a dangerous business when gangs are involved. These doe-eyed kids, with their sports team Starter jackets and fake gang signs, would be gobbled up in a New York minute by real gang members, with real gang attitudes and aggressions, brandishing real guns.

The bright spot here is that intervention will have the greatest success with clueless youths, as long as alternatives to gangs are made available.

COPYCAT GANGS

Gangs from a small city in Wisconsin may not have the same structure and leadership as the supergangs from Chicago. They may adopt the same dress, hand signs, symbols, and slang, but that is as far as it goes. For all practical purposes, a Vice Lord in Green Bay, Wisconsin, has nothing in common with a Vice Lord in Chicago. Small town gangs may be temporary in nature, consist of fifteen to twenty youths, and have no real hierarchical structure. They are likely to disband as soon as the community and law enforcement officials step in with swift anti-gang measures. This is not to say that "homegrown" gangs are any less destructive, however. Copycat gangs, as they are sometimes called, can be responsible for the same type of violence and crime associated with big city gangs, and should be treated with equal seriousness.

Chapter 5

WHY KIDS JOIN GANGS

Teenagers look at their parents and see their lives as humdrum and boring. Parents get up, go to work, pay bills, watch TV, go to bed, then repeat the process day in and day out. Except for a few outside activities—weekend chores, shopping, visits to friends, family outings—adult life appears pretty sedate. For a bored teenager, the lure of the gang is a powerful one. It promises adventure, intrigue, danger, a sense of the unknown—hunting down rival gang members while being hunted oneself.

But, in truth, being in a gang can also be boring. Gang members who don't go to school tend to sleep in late, sometimes until the afternoon. They get up, drink a pop, play a video game, then go out and "hang" with their homeboys, talking, bragging, and lying about past exploits, crimes, fights, and anything else that happens to be the current topic.

As day gives way to night, gang activity steps up. Parties, drive-by shootings, city lights, cops and robbers, hanging out—let the gang banging begin. The adrenaline rush gang members were after all along finally begins to flow. The fringe members don their gang jewelry and clothes, which was not permitted in school, and join the evening's gang activities.

Kids get a sense of identity and recognition from being in a gang. It sets them apart from their classmates and family; they achieve status among their peers. This is especially important if they are unable to succeed in other ways, such as through school, sports, or employment.

Kids get a sense of power by being in a gang. Alone, these youths feel small, powerless, inadequate. They lack direction. Belonging to a gang, however, makes them feel powerful, invincible. They have direction at last—the direction of the gang—and they finally feel a sense of belonging. This need for direction and belonging leaves kids vulnerable to the recruitment tactics of gangs.

GANG RECRUITMENT

Gangs recruit new members in many ways. While some intimidation still goes on, this seems to have given way to subtler methods. For example, gang members will describe all the good things gang life offers: money, friends, parties. Gone are the days when you could go down to the local department store and bring home a pair of Keds, Red Ball Jets, or Converse All Star sneakers for less than $15. Today's high-tech athletic footwear, sports team Starter jackets, and ten-karat gold jewelry cost a good sum of money. We're talking about a serious cash-flow problem. When known gang members go around flashing wads of bills, wearing gold jewelry, and dressing in designer sports apparel, gang life may seem too good to pass up. Gangs can bring immediate gratification to an economically disadvantaged youth. This can be a big draw, particularly in areas where jobs are low-paying or scarce. According to recent reports, the economic advantages to gang membership are so attractive that older males have begun to join. Their cash flow, of course, comes from less than honorable means—drug sales, gun running, extortion, robbery, burglary, and theft.

At first, with the promise of fortune dangling before them, many younger gang members unwittingly become pawns to the older members and are forced to carry out illegal activities. The older members know that if they commit the crimes themselves and are caught, they will certainly face jail terms, whereas younger members receive lighter sentences like probation and informal supervision. But time is rarely on the side of these young gang members. Just as they begin to see the gang's economic and hierarchical inequality, it's often too late. They find themselves on the way to juvenile prison.

At school, gang members recruit kids in more subtle ways. Members who attend school—and there are surprisingly many who do—are always on the lookout for kids who are picked on or shunned by other classmates. They befriend these kids, making them feel safe and accepted. Vulnerable kids see protection in a gang. There is power in numbers; if once they were picked on, now they are surrounded by dozens of gang members ready to back them up. For kids today, this backup, a cadre of instant friends, is one of the most appealing rewards of being in a gang.

When asked why they have joined a gang, many members reply that they feel like part of a family. In fact, gangs use this in their recruitment pitch: There is another family waiting for you—all you have to do is join. This pitch particularly appeals to children from single-parent families.

Actor and director Edward James Olmos directed and starred in the powerful major motion-picture about gang life, *American Me.* In conjunction with the film, he also produced, directed, and narrated an excellent anti-gang documentary called *Lives in Hazard,* using current and former gang members who received small acting parts in the movie. The title of his documentary refers to Big Hazard, the name of a gang in east Los Angeles.

In the film, Timmy, a member of Big Hazard, drives home a very important message:

> When I needed someone to play ball with, someone to play catch with, I always had older homeboys like Moon Dog, Flappers, . . . and them. They were around, and they were there for the kids, and they'd throw the baseball with me for an hour, half hour, even if it was five, ten minutes. Ya see, they became role models in my life. I didn't look at them as gang members. I didn't look at them as a bad person. I looked at them as somebody that paid attention to me.

This reasoning would come as no surprise to former gang member Nicky Cruz, now a minister working within his own outreach program in Colorado. During the writing of his book, *Code Blue,* Cruz telephoned police working with gang units in large cities and small towns across the nation to ask what they thought was the number one reason kids join gangs. Every police officer gave the same answer: the breakdown of the family. In many cases, Cruz reports, there is no positive male role model in single-parent homes. A youth at risk will often identify with the nearest male. Unfortunately, that particular male may be involved with gangs, or drugs. Even when both parents reside in the home, supervision and interaction may be inadequate, especially if both parents work outside the home. Also, if the parents themselves are involved with drugs or crime, or are verbally or physically abusive, the child may find friends with a similar background. The need for family, for those who love and accept us, is a powerful human need. Either we as parents supply it for our children, or the gangs will.

Recruitment is also influenced by a child's environment. If a child lives in a gang-infested neighborhood, he or she is expected to join a gang. This is where threats and intimidation play an important role. These children are motivated by fear. Many join to avoid harassment from neighborhood gangs, or to protect themselves against outside rival gangs coming into the area. Rival gangs entering a neighborhood frequently mistake innocent kids for gang members. Either way, these children are in danger.

Family environment plays an especially important role in the recruitment process, particularly when relatives themselves are in a gang. Among Hispanic gangs, it is not unusual for generations of family members to belong to the same gang—a family tradition, if you will. African American gangs, too, have shown a marked increase in second-generation gang members in the last decade. When a child is raised by a parent who is a gang member, the gang lifestyle is taught to and lived out in front of that child at a very early age.

Recruitment can also take place through gradual involvement in social events. Prospects, or non-gang members, are invited to parties where they may be given free drugs, booze, even sex. Of course, prospects must eventually "pay up" for all the free entertainment. Sometimes they find themselves wishing to continue that lifestyle. Either way, gang recruiters have their victims right where they want them—hooked.

Less insidious but no less dangerous are gang members who allow children to just hang out with them, acting tough. Even without full-blown membership, these kids experience their first sense of belonging and respect. The unspoken deal is this: If you want to be cool and hang with us, then you need to join us.

Gang recruitment is a gradual process. No one decides to join a gang overnight, just on a whim. If your child is verbalizing fears of the neighborhood or gang activity, listen. Ask your son or daughter if he or she has been approached by any gang members, or if anyone has tried to recruit him or her. Be direct. As a parent, you are not giving your child any new ideas that would encourage him or her to join a gang. Your child may not say it, but privately, he or she may be grateful you asked. If your child has been contacted by gang members, the time to respond is now.

Chapter 6

WHY AND HOW KIDS LEAVE GANGS

Kids leave gangs for many reasons and in many different ways. First, let's examine why a gang member would want to leave his or her gang. It is crucial to remember that no matter what the reasons are, it will be his or her fellow gang members' decision to either accept or reject those reasons.

Younger, newer gang members—the fringes and wanna-bes—may be frightened by the extreme violence displayed by hard-core members. It's one thing to slowly drive by a group of faceless individuals, discharging firearms into the darkness without seeing what or whom you've hit. It's another matter entirely to shoot someone up close, watching the pain in their eyes, or even worse, to witness a friend shredded by a barrage of gunfire. Such a personal look at violence can make even the most hard-core gang members blanch. Real-life violence is messy and gruesome—much more so that how it is portrayed on television. Some gang members get tired of the killing, the maiming, and the constant looking over their shoulder for enemies.

Younger gang members may find that their leader is really no better than an abusive parent, that they have simply traded one set of problems for another. The pain and fear older members often inflict on younger ones can be physical as well as mental, and younger members are usually unable to stand up against the abuse.

The discipline meted out by gang leaders can range from a BOS (Beat On Sight) order for a missed meeting, to execution for a major rule infraction. Such infractions are called V-Codes. The letter V stands for violation. Young gang members who want to go home for the night when they are tired might find themselves pushed into yet another gang activity, and they don't have a say in whether or not they participate. They must go with the flow.

As they get older, some gang members find that gang life no longer satisfies their needs. For many gang members, there comes a time when they realize they are no longer teenagers. They learn that there is more to life than just gang banging. This occurs most often when a gang member marries and sees an opportunity to settle down and raise a family. And just as some may realize that there's more to life, other gang members may realize that they are being used by older gang members to do their dirty work.

Or it can be as simple as a youth who, having joined a gang to escape family problems, begins to see those problems addressed and a healing process started. An outside influence, such as a counselor or member of the clergy, may be working with the family to restore relationships and help mend wounds. When this happens, the youth may want to rejoin his or her family. If an older family member belonging to a gang decides to break the cycle of involvement and denounces his or her own gang affiliation, the youth may see this as an opportunity to leave the gang as well.

Those are the whys. Now for the hows, which are far easier said than done.

Getting Out

Leaving a gang is not a simple process. Sometimes it can be dangerous. I would be remiss to the readers if I didn't stress that again. *Leaving a gang can be dangerous.*

A youth who is "jumped" or "courted" into a gang must sometimes go through the same process to leave it. This is called being "violated," "jumped out," "courted out," or "dropping the flag." Whatever the label, the process is the same as the initiation ritual, with one big difference: the beatings are usually much more severe. In Waukegan, a young man faced this beating when he decided to leave his gang some years back. He survived, but remained in a coma for fifty-eight days.

Gang members who decide to leave their gang put themselves at great risk, and they may put others in peril as well. Fellow gang members will sometimes retaliate against an entire family, particularly if they think the family is putting pressure on a resigning gang member to quit.

Youths who decide to leave a gang face some major obstacles:

- They are no longer protected by their own gang members from rival gang members who haven't heard about the resignation—and who won't stop to ask.
- Being jumped out doesn't protect the deactivated member from further harassment or beatings from the gang.
- The money and security of gang life are good. Alternatives, such as employment, are not always available on the outside.

Leaving a gang is not like choosing whether or not to do drugs. "Just Say No" doesn't always apply here. It used to be that if an individual wanted to get out of a gang, he or she just had to go down to the nearest military recruiting office and sign up. Not anymore. The military has higher education standards now, which makes most gang members ineligible. All is not lost, though. Youths can and do leave gangs, and there are a couple of methods that are often successful.

Fading Out

In all the years I've worked with gang members, I've found this technique to be the most successful. It is a gradual process where gang members find a job, get married, have children, and assume the necessary responsibilities for each. I have interviewed many ex-gang members in their late twenties and early thirties who have told me on more than one occasion, "I'm too old for that shit." When pressed, they have said they used to "bang," but now that they are married and have kids to feed, there is just no time. Of course, gang members must approach their homeboys and explain their reasons for wanting to leave, and it is up to the gang to accept or reject the request. But once a member is not wholeheartedly committed to gang life and is no longer as available as he or she once was, fellow gang members are more likely to let him or her out. That's the key. Gang members must decide to make themselves unavailable for gang activities. However, it should be remembered that depending on the particular structure of the gang, gang members who do not go along with gang activities may be violating one of their gang's laws, putting themselves in danger of punishment by the gang.

If gang structure is highly organized with numerous members, gang members will need a tightly-structured network of friends, family, and activities to help them stay clear of fellow gang members during the fading-out period. In loosely-structured gangs, fellow gang members may not actively look for members who disassociate themselves, and are likely to lose interest in pursuing members who never seem to be around.

Fading out seems to be the method females most often use to leave their gangs. As with male gangs, fellow members have the final say in whether to allow female gang members to leave. The responsibilities of having a baby, going back to school, or taking care of siblings are sometimes considered acceptable reasons.

There is one problem with fading out: it is not always an effective option for younger gang members. It is sometimes okay for older gang members to leave in good standing. After all, they've paid their dues, and if they are feared and respected by younger gang members, they may be allowed safe passage out of the gang. With younger gang members, however, the excuses of childbearing, marriage, or employment do not apply.

Younger members can still fade out—but this cannot be done without family and community support. When younger kids make themselves unavailable for gang activity, it lets the other members know that they have lost interest in gang life and no longer want to be a part of it. This is a gradual process. For example, a youth may find an after-school activity to keep him or herself busy until the majority of students have gone home. Perhaps a family member could pick the youth up from school at the end of the day. The key is intervention: youths must be given activities and alternatives to help them fade out of gang life. Kids cannot just stay at home, watch TV, and hope that other gang members won't call or stop by. Younger gang members must deliberately make themselves unavailable.

Outside activities, such as going to a church youth group or participating in YMCA or YWCA activities, are most helpful when adult friends or family members are there to participate. They can intervene if the youth happens to meet with a fellow gang member. Single-parent families can contact the Big Brothers and Big Sisters organization for help. This organization gives youths positive role models, activities, and alternatives to gang life. Families can also look for a gang outreach center in their town or city. These centers can be havens for individuals who want to leave a gang. Former gang members will be there to counsel youths on the dangers of gang participation while providing positive social activities.

Relocating

Some parents of gang members, fearing for their kids' lives, will send them to live with a relative in another city or state. Unfortunately, if children do not want to leave gang life, they may start their own gang, or hook up with an existing gang in the area. Relocation must not be forced. It only works when the child wants, and is ready, to leave the gang.

Again, it must be stressed that gangs have been known to go after entire families if those families are encouraging their sons or daughters to drop out of the gang. Families must have a carefully thought out plan of action. Some of the larger metropolitan areas have gang outreach programs sponsored by police, civic groups, and churches, which can assist families in relocating and securing new jobs while maintaining their anonymity. Drastic times call for drastic measures. Parents should check with their local government officials or police probation departments for a gang outreach program near them. If none is available, speak out. Enough concerned parents, citizens, and educators may galvanize a local government, church, or civic organization into sponsoring this sort of program.

The most important step in getting a child out of a gang is this: Parents must communicate with their children. Many younger gang members do want to get out, but are frightened and don't know where to turn. If your child is in a gang, ask if he or she wants to leave it. The answer may be no. Keep asking. Eventually, the answer might be yes. Your child may grow tired of gang life with all its dangerous trappings and look to you for assistance. This would not be the time to turn a deaf ear. Look beyond your own anger at your child's gang involvement. Open communication may save your child.

Part Three

Children and Gang Behavior

Knowing the Signs

Chapter 7

GENERAL GANG IDENTIFIERS

Before assuming your child is a gang member based on the style of clothing he or she wears, it is important to remember that just because one of the following identifiers is present, it doesn't necessarily mean your child is in a gang. The best and safest thing to do is look for several identifiers. For example, if your child has a tattoo, wears gang jewelry, and has unusual markings on his or her clothing, then he or she may be involved in gang activity. If you know for certain that your child is not involved with gangs, but wears clothing and jewelry associated with the gang lifestyle, then he or she is making some extremely poor fashion choices. The best rule to follow is this: If your child displays three or more identifiers, be aware that he or she may be in a gang and investigate the matter further.

African American Gangs Identifiers

Right/Left Rule

The Folk and People gangs use direction—in other words, they emphasize the right or left side of their body—to represent affiliation. For example, Folks display clothing and accessories on the right. This includes tilting a hat or cap to the right, wearing gang-colored shoelaces on the right shoe, moving belt buckles to the right, wearing gloves and earrings on the right side, hanging handkerchiefs or bandannas from the right pocket or attaching them to the right leg, and painting two fingernails on the right hand with gang colors. People display their accessories in the same manner, but use the left side.

Folk and People gangs will use this right/left rule not only with the clothing and accessories they wear, but also with their hand signs, tattoos, and even their stance. For example: gang members affiliated with the Folks may fold their arms over the right side of their body, keep their right hand inside of their right pocket, lean their body to the right, tattoo their right arm, or throw their hand signals from the right side.

Despite affiliations with the Folks and the People, however, Crips and Bloods do not necessarily display in this manner. It depends on their region. For example, in Los Angeles, Crips and Bloods may not use direction at all. In Minneapolis, Crips will display on the left, in order to differentiate themselves from the Disciples, who also wear blue but display on the right. Bloods will display on the right to distinguish themselves from the Vice Lords, who also wear red but display on the left. Check with local law enforcement officials to determine how gangs in your area use direction to represent affiliation.

Shoes

Most African American gang members, both male and female, favor expensive, modern, high-tech designs in athletic footwear. Gone are the old-fashioned canvas sneakers that were popular in the sixties and seventies. Gang members will sometimes color the tongue of their shoe with their gang colors or mark it with their initials: VL for Vice Lords, BGD for Black Gangster Disciple, 4CH for 4 Corner Hustlers, and so forth. And of course, the right/left rule applies: Right tongue up, left tongue down generally means an affiliation with the Folks; left tongue up, right tongue down, with the People.

British Knights footwear, which carries the initials BK, is popular among the Crips. They use these initials to mean Blood Killer. Gang members from the People Nation will wear Converse athletic shoes because of the five-point star on the side. They sometimes color this five-point star with gang colors.

Shoelaces

Parents and educators should pay close attention to the way children wear their shoelaces. The following signify some gang affiliations:

- People Nation gangs will sometimes lace their shoes up to only five holes.
- Folk Nation gangs will sometimes lace their shoes up to only six holes.
- Gangs often display their colors on both their shoes and shoelaces. For example, if a gang's colors are blue and black, a gang member may wear black athletic shoes with blue laces.
- Some gangs wear two sets of different colored laces in either the right or left shoe, and occasionally in both, to show gang affiliation. For example, if a gang's color are red and yellow, a gang member might wear athletic shoes with both red and yellow laces.

Pants

African American gangs often wear their pants low, over the waist. This is called "sagging," and is a popular fad among gang members and non-gang youths alike.

- Pant leg cuffs rolled up on the right side represent the Folk Nation. Pant leg cuffs rolled up on the left side signify the People.
- Gang members often color the inside of their pant pockets with gang colors. Folks pull their right pockets inside out, whereas People display on the left side.
- Some gang members wear overalls, with one strap unbuttoned on either the right or the left side to show their affiliation.

Sports Team Starter Jackets and Sweatshirts

The Starter jacket is one of the easiest ways to identify a youth with possible gang affiliations. Much has been written about gangs wearing sports team jackets. Gangs will adopt teams, professional and collegiate, for two reasons: if the gang colors are the same as the team colors, and if the sports team logo looks like, or can be altered to look like, their gang symbol.

Parents and educators should be concerned if a child is sporting a new Starter jacket and has never expressed an interest in professional or collegiate sports. The same can be said if the child is associating with kids who wear identical sports team apparel.

Some gang members will wear a hooded sweatshirt with a jacket, usually a sports team Starter jacket, over it. The hood usually hangs out over the collar of the jacket. The thing to note here is the color of the hood in relation to the color of the jacket. For example, a member from the gang Insane Deuces may wear a green, hooded sweatshirt under a black jacket. Parents should take note of such color combinations and refer to the table beginning on page 81 (as well as their local law enforcement agency) for information on gang colors. Your child may not be in a gang, but may unwittingly leave the house wearing the wrong color combination. Gang members could mistake the child for someone who is "flying their colors," or they might think he or she is a member of a rival gang.

Hats and Caps

The hat or cap is the second most obvious identifier. The way a person wears a hat or baseball cap—tilted to the right or the left, for example—can indicate a gang affiliation. In addition, gang members sometime turn their hats completely around, wearing them backward with the adjustment strap lying flat against the forehead. If the hat is perfectly aligned in the middle, it may mean the person has no gang affiliation. Gang members sometimes adjust their caps so that the logo is prominent on either the right or the left side. The same can be done with a knit stocking cap. Check your child's hat or baseball cap to see if the logo has been altered in any way, for example, if letters have been added or deleted or if colors have been changed. Both the underside and the outer portion of the cap should be closely inspected for any unusual writing, markings, symbols, or street names.

Also, look closely at the area where the brim and the body of the cap are sewn together. There is usually a small, half-inch strip of material where some gang members have been known to hide their street names or gang affiliations. This strip of material should be pulled down to check for any writing or symbols.

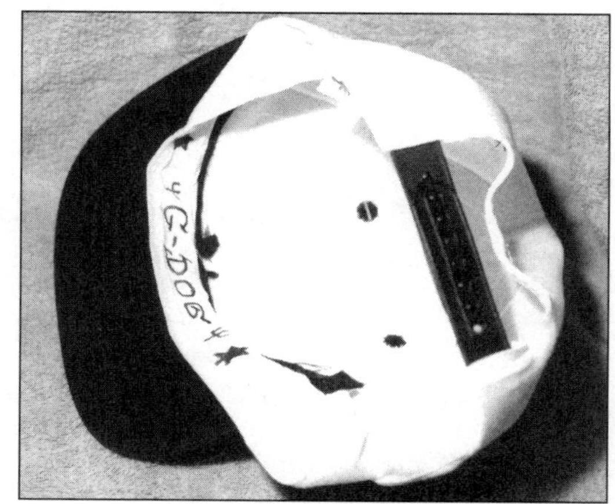

At first glance, this cap appears to have no gang markings. But hidden beneath the strip of material where the brim meets the body of the cap is the wearer's street name, "G-Dog," and a few gang symbols. When checking your child's hat, be sure to pull down this 3/4" strip to look for gang markings.

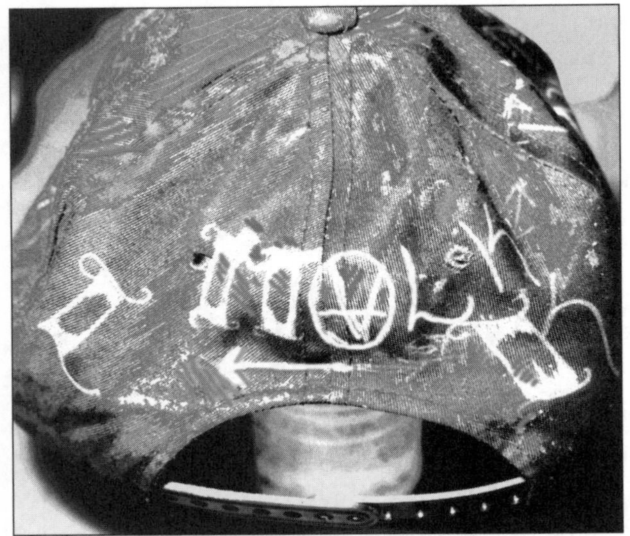

The wearer of this cap is a member of the Latin Kings. Note the upside-down OA insignia in the center. This is meant to insult their rival gang, Orchestra Albany.

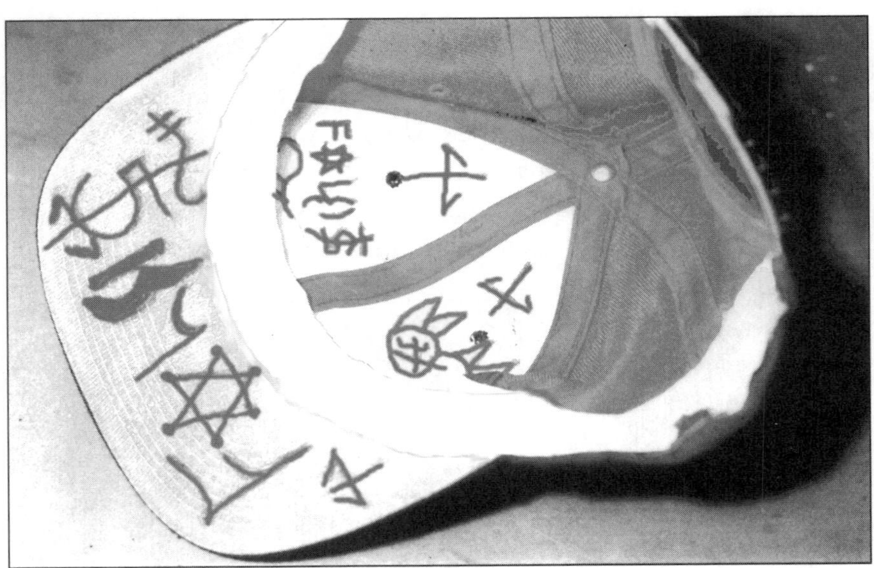

The upside-down numeral 5, the six-point star, and the upturned pitchforks on this hat indicate that the wearer is a member of a Folk gang. Parents should always check inside their child's hat for gang symbols.

Hair and Eyebrows

African American male gang members currently wear their hair very short, or they shave their heads. As with most fashions that are popular among young people, however, this is likely to change. Some gang members place colored rubber bands in sections of their hair, the colors representing gang affiliation. Other gang members place colored beads or a small streak of hair coloring on either the right or left side of the head, depending on their gang affiliation. Some members cut designs into their hair, a trend that used to be popular among rap singers and athletes Look for such symbols as pitchforks, arrows, and crowns.

Female gang members also wear their hair according to current fashions, placing colored beads, barrettes, hair wraps (called scrunchies), and rubber bands in their hair. Again, the colors of these accessories will represent gang affiliation.

Gang members will sometimes shave vertical lines into their eyebrows to show affiliation, leaving five or six tufts of hair. Often only the right or left eyebrow will be shaved.

African American Female Gang Clothing

Like male gang members, African American female gang members generally dress according to current styles. Although some female gang members wear clothing similar to their male counterparts, they tend to use additional accessories to set their gang apart from others. These include belts, sweaters, and shoes, all with corresponding gang colors.

Tattoos

Tattoos, which indicate one's loyalty to the gang, are simply an extension of gang graffiti. They are found primarily on the hands, arms, chest, back, legs and neck. A teardrop tattooed on a gang member's cheek has a couple of different meanings. Teardrops can represent the number of fellow gang members who have been killed, or, if the gang member is an enforcer, the number of rival gang members he or she has killed. In some gangs, the outline of a teardrop represents the death of a fellow gang member, whereas a solid teardrop indicates the murder of a rival. The right/left rule applies, of course: teardrops on the right cheek represent a Folk affiliation, teardrops on the left signify People.

Other tattoos, usually found on the arm, include pitchforks, crowns, and gang initials. While extremely popular among male gang members, tattoos are not generally used by African American female gang members.

Automobile Air Fresheners

In the last few years, some gangs have begun using automobile air fresheners that are shaped like crowns. The Latin Kings, Imperial Gangsters, and other gangs who use a crown in their symbol will place these air fresheners on their dashboards and in the back windows of their cars. Unfortunately, many unsuspecting citizens also use these automobile air fresheners without knowing the risk. Cars carrying crown-shaped air fresheners are a prime target for vandalism.

Hispanic Gang Identifiers

Shoes

Like African American gang members, both male and female Hispanic gang members wear the latest athletic shoes available. Some members of the Latin Kings will wear Converse shoes with the bottom portion of the logo blacked out. This gives the star the appearance of a crown, the Latin King symbol.

Pants and Shorts

Hispanic gangs usually wear Dickie brand pants, either in black or khaki, with a waistband that is often two sizes too large. This sizing allows for the "sagging" style that is so popular today, where the pants drop slightly over the buttocks to reveal boxer shorts underneath. I visited one home where the youth's pants sagged so much that he had to hold them up by the waistband whenever he tried to walk.

Gang members wear shorts in the sagging style as well, so that the pant legs hang below their knees. It's not unusual to see a one- to three-inch gap between the bottom of the shorts and top of the socks. These styles, of course, are also popular among non-gang youths.

Shirts

Hispanic gang members favor white tee shirts, which are usually sleeveless to help show off tattoos and muscle tone. Pendleton shirts are also popular among Hispanic gangs. The shirts are usually worn one to three sizes too large. Oversized clothing serves two purposes: it makes a youth look larger, and it conceals weapons.

Hats

Stocking caps are very popular among Hispanic gangs and are worn year round. Because many gang members shave their heads or wear their hair closely cropped, the stocking caps can be worn during the summer months with no discomfort.

Like African American gangs, Hispanic gangs will write gang symbols on their sports caps. Inspect your child's hat carefully for any suspicious markings. Be sure to check underneath the cap, and look beneath the strip of material where the brim meets the body. For more on hats and gang markings, see pages 59–60.

Hair

Hispanic male gang members either shave their heads or wear their hair very short. Many gang members (and non-gang members) who sport shaved heads leave a small ponytail or tuft of hair in the back. Mustaches and goatees are also very popular among these gangs.

Hispanic female gang members generally wear their hair long and full with their bangs flipped up and held in place with styling gel. They will occasionally color their hair a reddish dark brown, although many Hispanic women who are not affiliated with gangs do this, too.

Hispanic Female Gang Clothing

Hispanic female gang members often wear the same clothing as their male counterparts—Pendleton shirts and khaki pants, for example. Very seldom do Hispanic gang girls wear dresses. Their clothing is usually very dark in color, most often black, brown, or blue. Bandannas with gang colors are also quite common, and can be worn around the head or used as belts.

Makeup

Makeup is an integral part of a Hispanic female gang member's appearance. The facial base is usually thick and light in color. Lipstick, eye shadow, eye liner, eyebrow pencils, and fingernail polish are usually black or very dark brown. The dark color against the light facial base makes for a striking appearance.

Magazines

One identifier that is indisputably gang related is the magazine *Teen Angels*. This magazine, which originates in California, has been around for a number of years. The magazine itself is expensive ($6.95) and contains numerous ink drawings and photographs of gangs. It also includes pen pal letters, photos of incarcerated Hispanic gang members, and gang dedications listing gang members' monikers in honor roll fashion. The magazine carries a number of articles about legal issues and other topics of interest to its readers. There are also plenty of advertisements from different businesses in the town where it originates. Distributed nationally, *Teen Angels* is aimed exclusively at gangs, and there's not a lot parents or anyone else can do about it. The magazine proudly proclaims its membership with the American Civil Liberties Union, which, incidentally, advertises in the magazine and lists its offices in the western states.

Teen Angels has been found among African American gangs as well, so its readership is not exclusively Hispanic.

Tattoos

Tattoos are very popular among Hispanic male gang members and may be located anywhere on the body. Members will tattoo the name of their gang, as well as a name or number to represent the street or area where they come from. Members of the 18th Street gang, for example, may have a Gothic or Roman numeral 18 on their forearm or elsewhere. The numeral 18 represents both the name of the gang and the name of the street they are from. A gang member from the southern area of California may have a tattoo of the number 13. The numbers 13 and 14 represent which side of Bakersfield, California, a gang member is from. The number 13, either on its own or in conjunction with the word *sur,* means that the gang member is from southern California, or below Bakersfield. The number 14, sometimes written with the word *norte,* indicates the gang member is from northern California, or above Bakersfield. (For more information on how gangs use numbers, see Appendix Two.)

Many hard-core Hispanic female gang members also have tattoos. Among the most popular are their street name, gang affiliation, and boyfriend's name. These tattoos are usually located on the shoulder, around the ankle, on the back, or across the chest. A tattoo of a rosary or a crucifix may also be found across the breasts or on the back. Either of these signifies that the member will give up her life for the gang and its neighborhood.

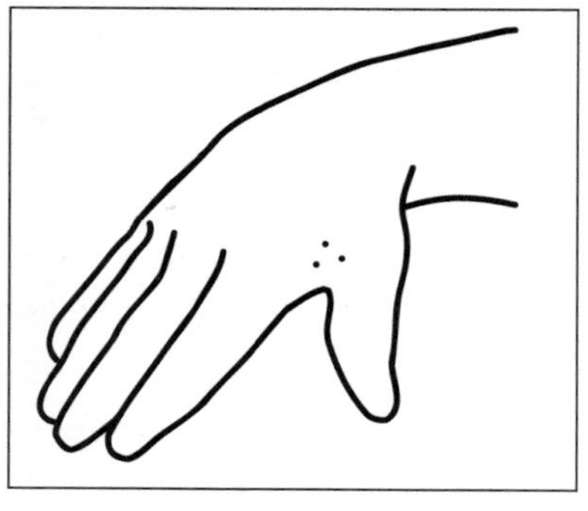

"Mi Vida Loca"

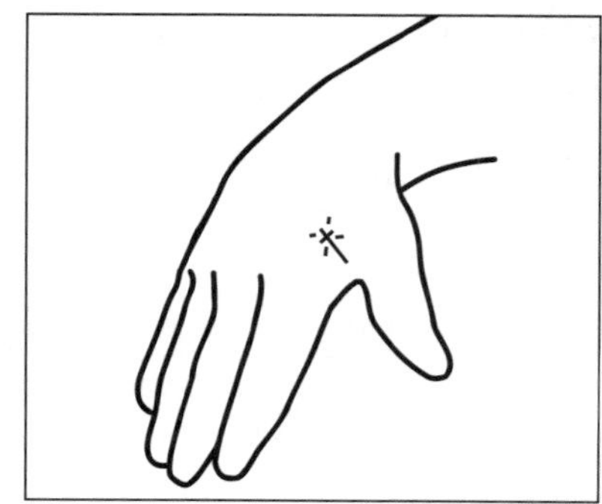

Pachuco cross

Both male and female gang members sometimes have a three-dot pyramid tattooed on the webbing between their thumb and forefinger, elsewhere on their hand, or on their face. The three dots represent "Mi Vida Loca" or "my crazy life." Another popular tattoo is the pachuco cross, which may also be found anywhere on the hand or face, but most often on the webbing between the thumb and forefinger. Pachuco gang members of the 1940s wore this tattoo to identify themselves, and today's Hispanic gangs have adopted it as well.

Southeast Asian Gang Identifiers

Clothing

Initially, Southeast Asian gang members wore white shirts, black or white pants, and white or black jackets. This style of dress set them apart from the rest of the gangs. In some parts of the country, this "uniform" can still be found. For the most part, though, gang members tend to dress according to current fashion. Male gang members may wear saggy pants, emulating African American and Hispanic gang members. Some have begun to incorporate the gang colors belonging to the Crips and Bloods. Southeast Asian gang members choose clothes that blend in with the surroundings to avoid drawing attention to themselves, especially from the police.

In addition to wearing the current fashions, Southeast Asian female gang members occasionally wear clothes that set them apart from the non-gang Asian girls in the school or neighborhood. This clothing often includes leather skirts, black stockings, and high-heeled shoes.

Hair

Most Southeast Asian gang members cut their hair according to current fashion. Like Hispanic members, Southeast Asian female members tend to wear long, full hair with their bangs flipped up. A few male gang members shave their heads, leaving a knob or tail of hair in the back. Some shave their heads to change their looks, particularly after committing a crime. Others use hair spray, egg whites, or corn starch to change their hairstyles, all of which can be brushed or washed out easily.

Parents should watch their children to see if they are in possession of quick hair color spray. Called "hair dust," this product is sprayed onto the hair to temporarily change its color. For example, before a crime takes place, a gang member sprays the color red into his or her hair. The victim later describes this individual to the police, who begin looking for a redhead. After the offender has left the crime scene, however, he or she combs out the color in a matter of minutes, changing his or her appearance once again. Other temporary hair colors can be shampooed out, and most are easily purchased throughout the year. These products are frequently used in Halloween costumes, but if Halloween is months away and your child is in possession of temporary hair coloring, it might be a good idea to ask some questions.

Makeup

Southeast Asian female gang members have emulated Hispanic female gangs in their makeup: light facial base with thick, dark lipstick, eye liner, and eye shadow.

Tattoos

Southeast Asian individuals who do not belong to a gang will sometimes wear such traditional tattoos as dragons, Buddha symbols, flying eagles, sailing ships, and panthers. But if your child comes home with a tattoo, and his friends or associates have the same tattoo, this may be a sign of gang involvement.

Male gang members will sometimes tattoo their name, street moniker, or gang name using either English or their native language. As with hair color products, these tattoos may be temporary; sometimes they are only drawn with a pen. This is often done to avoid identification.

Hard-core Southeast Asian gang members may have dots, circles, or the letter T tattooed or burned into their skin in groups of three, four, or five. The grouping of three dots, circles, or T's refers to the Vietnamese saying, "Toi O Can Gica," or "I don't care about anything." These three burn marks can also represent "my crazy life," much the same way Hispanic gangs use "Mi Vida Loca." Burn marks can be located almost anywhere on the body, but the stomach and the back of the hand seem to be most popular. Although burn marks may be tattooed on the skin, actual burns prove an individual's toughness and craziness. Generally, if younger or hard-core Southeast Asian gang members want to be viewed as tougher or crazier than the others, they will display a larger number of burn marks.

The grouping of four dots, circles or T's stands for Tinh (love), Tien (money), Tu (prison), and Tai (crime). The fifth, if used, stands for Thu (revenge). T's are usually drawn in Gothic style and can be found on the upper portion of the arm, across the neck, or on the back of the hand. Instead of T's, the words are sometimes written out or displayed as 4xT or 5xT.

Another method of tattooing is with cigarette burns. The markings have definite meaning, and parents and educator should watch for them. Five cigarette burn marks in a circular pattern stand for the Vietnamese words "Tu" (for), "Hai" (all directions), "Giai" (group), "Huyhn" (friends), and "De" (brothers). Together these five marks generally mean "a group of good friends."

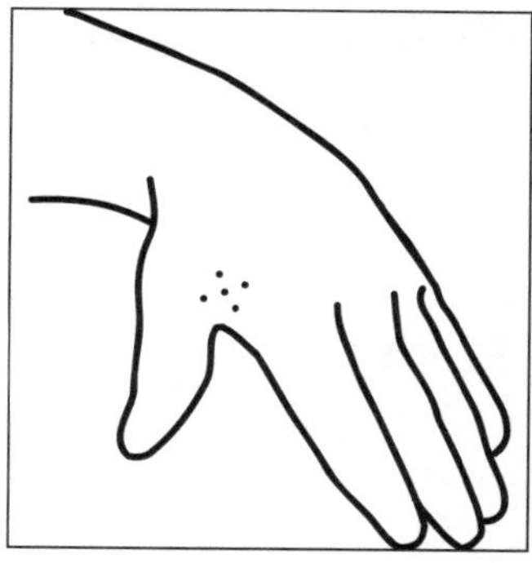

To Southeast Asian gangs, five dots represent Tinh (love), Tien (money), Tu (prison), Tai (crime), and Thu (revenge). Five dots in a circle, however, would mean "a group of good friends."

Southeast Asian female gang members tattoo themselves by cutting or burning designs into their skin. The tattooed areas are generally covered with clothing and may contain the same types of tattoos as the Hispanic gangs use, for example, a boyfriend's name, gang affiliation, or street name.

Skinhead Gang Identifiers

Shoes

Imported from England, Doctor Marten boots (also called Doc Martens) are the number one choice among Skinheads. Doc Martens are considered authentic, coming directly from the European Skinhead movement. If they are unavailable, however, or if cost is a factor, Skinheads will sometimes substitute surplus army boots. Although there are several colors to choose from, the most popular color is black.

Skinheads favor steel-toed Doc Martens because they do more damage in a fight. Gang members tend to opt for the boots with the most laces, as well. Some boots reach almost to the knees of the wearer, and those with a large number of laces are perceived as more menacing when the pants are rolled up or tucked in. To the Skinhead, image is everything.

The color of the bootlaces is also significant. White laces, for example, denote white pride or white power. Red laces signify that the wearer is ready to spill his or her own blood for the cause, or they identify the wearer as a neo-Nazi. Green laces indicate that the Skinhead is a gay basher, and yellow means that the wearer has recently injured someone.

Pants

Skinheads prefer blue or black jeans and military camouflage. While at school or at work, they generally wear their pants over their boots to avoid drawing unnecessary attention to themselves. When Skinheads want to let someone know that they're Skinheads, they roll their pant cuffs up to highlight their boots.

Jackets

Skinheads often wear U.S. Air Force flight jackets. The jacket comes in three colors: black, green, and brown. It is a Skinhead's most prized possession, and the most revealing. For example, patches or drawings of swastikas, the KKK (Ku Klux Klan) symbol, lightning bolts, and the Celtic cross denote which affiliation he or she has an interest in. Grouped letters, too, can be significant—namely, WAR (White Aryan Resistance) and AYM (Aryan Youth Movement).

Braces

Americans call them suspenders, the British call them braces. Unlike Doc Martens or the Air Force flight jacket, which are essential attire, braces are an optional accessory. Some Skinheads never wear braces, some wear them all the time, and some just wear them at meetings and demonstrations.

The color of the braces will usually have the same meaning as the color of the bootlaces. At one time, Skinheads wore their braces down, or off the shoulder, when there was about to be a physical confrontation. Today's Skinheads choose many ways to wear braces, and only they understand the meaning of each.

Female Skinhead Clothing

Female Skinheads wear the same Doc Marten boots and flight jackets decorated with Nazi insignia. But unlike the male Skinheads, female Skinheads do not generally wear braces.

Tattoos

A Skinhead will often tattoo symbols such as SS death heads, Viking warriors, barbed wire, swastikas, and Iron Crosses on the neck, arms, hands, face, and even on the shaved head. Words such as "Skins," "White Power," and "Nazi" might also be found next to these symbols.

Hair

The name itself—Skinhead—is derived from the practice of shaving one's head. The sight of a shaved head is a real attention getter—exactly what a Skinhead thrives on. Parents should note, however, that some Skinheads will allow their hair to grow out to lessen the negative attention. Parents should then look for the other identifiers in this chapter to determine if their child might be involved in the Skinhead movement.

Female Skinheads rarely shave their heads, but they do tend to cut their hair in a conservative fashion. Some female Skinheads bleach their hair, promoting the Aryan look and signifying their allegiance to an all-white race.

Graffiti

Parents and educators should always be on the lookout for graffiti, which may be written on school notebooks and other personal items. While the graffiti of African American and Hispanic gangs can be complex, even artful, the same cannot be said for that of Skinheads. Skinhead graffiti is usually crude, poorly drawn, and simple. Messages and symbols leave no doubt as to their authorship: racist epithets, Nazi symbols, and other violent images. This graffiti is often placed on Jewish synagogues, African American churches, and businesses owned by either of these groups. It is written on the walls of the buildings for the world to see; in cases of burglary, it marks the crime scene for a more personal affront. The police and legislators have appropriately titled these terrible deeds "hate crimes."

Literature/Posters/Fliers

What Skinheads lack in artistic flair, they more than make up for in their literature. There is probably no better way for a Skinhead to spread propaganda than to release a hate-filled poster or flier into

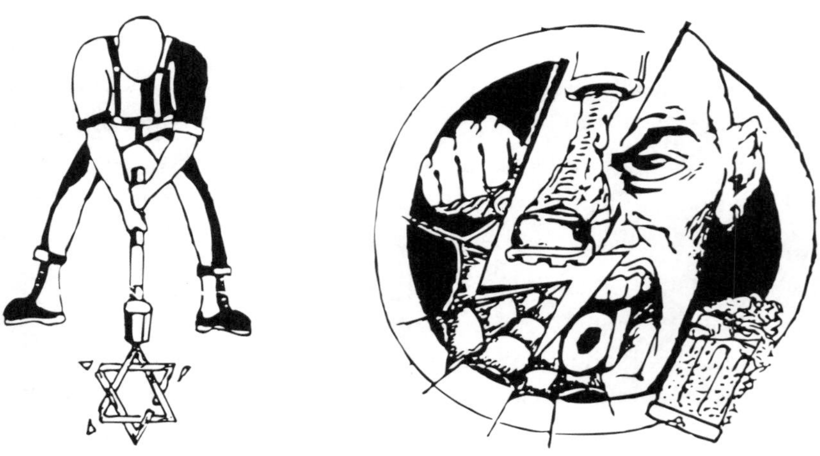

Skinhead artwork

the hands of the general public. Distributed on street corners and at demonstrations, or placed on the windshield of cars, these are the Skinheads' handbills of hate. Some include artwork. The artwork itself is shared from group to group, and the same artwork may be used for years. Art varies from the crude to the expertly drawn.

Skinhead artwork

Through fliers and posters, Skinheads let the public know what they perceive is happening to this country. Geared toward the impressionable young, these fliers are used to "educate" others and perpetuate the Skinheads' twisted logic and viewpoints.

Fliers and posters are also used as recruitment tools. Some carry the name of the local Skinhead group, along with a post office box address to which individuals can write for more information or make a financial contribution.

Music

The music Skinheads listen to ranges from heavy metal to "white power" music. Parents should be on the lookout for tapes, records, and CDs by groups whose names may be associated with Skinhead or neo-Nazi ideology. Many of the recordings are imported from Europe by white supremacy groups. These albums can be difficult to find in the United States, and Skinheads will often settle for bootleg copies of the originals.

Imported from the United Kingdom are such groups as Sudden Impact, Elite Terror, No Remorse, The Klansmen, Brutal Attack, Public Enemy (not to be confused with the African American rap group of the same name), Skullhead, Black Flag, and the most successful group, Screwdriver, which brought the Skinhead movement to the United States. Direct from France come groups called Brutal Combat, Warrior Kids, and Evil Skins.

In the United States, we now have homegrown bands with such names as Doc Martens, The Kicker Boys, Bound For Glory, Anti Heroes, Final Solution, Prisoner of Peace, White Pride, US Chaos, Nigger Nigger, and Rahowa. The head of the band Rahowa has his own label, Resistance Records. He also publishes the newsletter *Resistance,* a catalog containing information for ordering other Skinhead music.

Weapons

For the most part, Skinheads use simple and straightforward weapons—knives, clubs (some with protruding spikes or nails), hand guns, and sawed-off shotguns, to name a few. Because Skinheads are not financially motivated and don't generally have the financial advantage that other gangs have, automatic weapons like Uzis and Mac-10s are usually out of their price range. Besides, automatic weapons would be inconsistent with the Skinhead image. Whereas African American, Hispanic, and Caucasian gangs do drive-bys, randomly spraying gunshots into a crowd, Skinheads prefer to be up close and personal, hearing the sound of bones cracking beneath the blows of a baseball bat. That kind of sick satisfaction is lost if you're anonymously shooting someone from half a block away.

Educators who come across any of these weapons should notify the appropriate authorities. Parents finding such weapons may wish to consult local law enforcement officials for advice on their proper disposal.

Computers

Desktop publishing and on-line "chat rooms" are the wave of the future for budding Skinheads. Working-class Skinheads are less likely to own a personal computer, of course. But computers are common among Skinheads from middle- and upper-middle class families—especially since the early 1990s, when the cost of computers plummeted.

With a good used computer, which generally starts at under $500, and an inkjet printer capable of producing graphics, a Skinhead can churn out any number of fliers to suit the group's needs and ideology. Skinheads want to spread their word, and computers are their most effective tool. The use of computers sets them apart from the other gangs.

With a computer and modem, a Skinhead can access neo-Nazi chat rooms and bulletin boards, the catalog *Resistance,* and many other racist publications and organizations on the Internet. The old adage "like seeks like" applies—white supremacy groups, Skinheads, and neo-Nazis all take to these on-line services.

Parents, pay attention to your children's nocturnal tapping at the computer keyboard. Find out if it's homework, or something a bit more ominous.

The following graphics were downloaded from a website called Stormfront. They are but a small sample of the Skinhead/neo-Nazi images available on the Internet.

W·A·R
WHITE PRIDE
WORLD WIDE

TAGGER GANG IDENTIFIERS

Clothing

Tagger clothing is generally nothing special: baseball caps, oversized pants, and flannel shirts, with knapsacks and army fatigues (the large pockets make it easy to carry numerous cans of spray paint). Parents should examine clothing carefully for any sign or smell of paint to determine if their child is involved with a Tagger group.

Paint

Many cities and towns have ordinances forbidding the sale of spray paint to minors, so paint is often obtained by shoplifting. Taggers use lots of paint—a dozen cans in one night is not uncommon—and paint has to be stored somewhere. Parents should look in the basement, attic, garage, and tool box for large numbers of spray paint cans.

Photographs

Taggers take pride in their work. They know their art may last only a few days before it is destroyed. They take photographs of their work and place them in photo albums to show off to friends and other Taggers. These items are likely to be well hidden, so search your child's room and other areas of the house carefully if you think your child may be involved in this type of activity.

Magazines

A number of underground magazines are aimed at the graffiti artist. Because graffiti is considered "art" to Taggers and "vandalism" to law enforcement officials, these magazines are hardly ever found on the corner newsstand. Instead, *On The Go, Can Control, Skills, Tight,* and *Twelve Ounce Prophet* are usually sold by subscription only and have a nationwide distribution. These magazines have been out there for quite a while, and they're growing. *Tight* was established in 1983, for example, and *Can Control* boasts a circulation of 20,000.

Chapter 8

SYMBOLS, GRAFFITI, AND JEWELRY

Gang Symbols

Symbols have distinct meanings to different gangs and are useful in identifying specific gang affiliations. There are literally thousands of gangs throughout the country, each with several to dozens of symbols. Smaller gangs, for example, may have their own separate symbols, yet they also incorporate symbols of national gangs into their clothing, tattoos, and graffiti. And gangs with alliances to the Folk and People Nations have a number of symbols to choose from. The following list contains symbols used by the two main factions, the Folks and the People. This list is only a sample, however, and parents and educators should contact the police or probation department in their area for information on specific local gangs and their symbols.

Parents should carefully examine their child's clothing for gang symbols and, if they find any, address the issue immediately. If a child is drawing gang symbols on his or her schoolbooks, this should also be of concern. Even if a child is not in a gang, a simple gang doodle drawn on a notebook will attract immediate attention not only from school officials, but also from rival gang members.

The Folk Nation

Typically, Folks either spell out their gang name or use the six-point star to identify themselves. The six-point star, the Star of David, represents the six principles of King David: Life, Love, Loyalty, Knowledge, Understanding, and Wisdom. The six-point star is incorporated into many of the symbols used by gangs affiliated with the Folk Nation. Other symbols include dice, swords, pitchforks (which always point upward), a devil's tail or horns, winged hearts, backward swastikas, crowns with rounded edges, and Playboy bunnies with a bent ear. Although each gang wears its own color combination, many Folk gangs will wear black and silver as well.

The People Nation

The main symbol of the People Nation is the five-point star. The five-point star represents five principles: Love, Truth, Peace, Freedom, and Justice. The other symbols used by gangs affiliated with the People Nation include crescent moons, crosses, champagne glasses, staffs or canes, Playboy bunnies with a straight ear, pyramids, five-point crowns, and top hats.

Downward-pointing pitchforks frequently appear in People graffiti. The pitchfork is actually a Folk Nation symbol. When People display this symbol upside down, they are insulting the Folks.

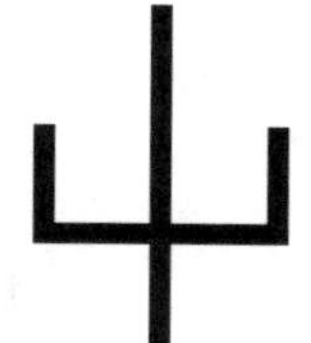

Pitchfork (symbol of the Folk Nation)

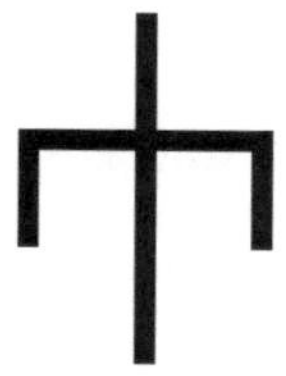

Downward pitchfork (used by People gangs to insult the Folks)

Symbols of Gangs Affiliated with the Folk and People Nations

Gang Name	Color(s)	Symbol(s)
Ambrose (Folk Nation)	black and light blue	Helmet with plumes and spear; script initial A
Ashland Vikings (Folk Nation)	black and green	6-point star; Viking helmet
Bishops (People Nation)	black and copper, black and brown	Gothic letter B; bishop's cross
Black Disciples (Folk Nation)	black and blue	*see* Black Gangster Disciples
Black Gangster Disciples (Folk Nation)	black and blue	Initials BGD, GD, or BOS (Brothers of the Struggle), and crossed pitchforks; 6-point star
Black P Stone Nation (People Nation)	black, red, and green	*see* El Rukns
Bloods (People Nation)	red, sometimes gold	5-point star
Brothers of the Struggle (Folk Nation)	black and blue	*see* Black Gangster Disciples
C-Notes (Folk Nation)	white and green. white and red	Dollar sign; 6-point star
Campbell Boys (Folk Nation)	red and blue	Devil's horns; pitchforks
Conservative Vice Lords (People Nation)	black and gold, black and red	*see* Vice Lords
Crips (Folk Nation)	blue	The word CRIP

Cullerton Deuces (People Nation)	black, gray, and white	The two of spades; dice showing two dots or the numeral 2
Ebony Vice Lords (People Nation)	black and gold, black and red	*see* Vice Lords
El Rukns (People Nation)	black, red, and green	5-point star; crescent moon with 5-point star; pyramid with crescent moon; numeral 7; initials BPSN (for Black P Stone Nation) inside a circle; pyramid with an eye
4 Corner Hustlers (People Nation)	black and gold, black and red	*see* Vice Lords
Future Stones (People Nation)	black and orange	5-point diamond; pyramid with twenty-one bricks; the numeral 5
Gangster Disciples (Folk Nation)	black and blue	*see* Black Gangster Disciples
Gangster Stone Vice Lords (People Nation)	black and gold, black and red	*see* Vice Lords
Gaylords (People Nation)	black and gray, black and light blue	Cross with a wreath; Initials GL
Harrison Gents (Folk Nation)	black and purple	Two crossed canes with a top hat; initials HG
Imperial Gangsters (Folk Nation)	black and pink	Crown with a rounded edge; pitchforks; pink panther; initials IG
Imperial Insane Vice Lords (People Nation)	black and gold, black and red	*see* Vice Lords
Insane Deuces (People Nation)	black and green	The two of spades; dice showing two dots or the numeral 2

Insane Satan Disciples (Folk Nation)	black and yellow	*see* Satan Disciples
Insane Unknowns (People Nation)	black and white	White-robed figure with rifle; cross with initials UNKNS
Insane Vice Lords (People Nation)	black and gold, black and red	*see* Vice Lords
La Raza (Folk Nation)	green, white, and red	Eagle; Mexican flag; initials LRZ
Latin Brothers (People Nation)	black and purple, black and white	Roman helmet; initials LBN
Latin Counts (People Nation)	black and red	Knight's helmet; initials LC
Latin Disciples (Folk Nation)	black and blue	*see* Maniac Latin Disciples
Latin Dragons (Folk Nation)	black and green	6-point star; fire-breathing dragon
Latin Eagles (Folk Nation)	black and gray	Eagle's head; gold eagle in flight with initials LE
Latin Kings (People Nation)	black and gold	5- or 3-point crown; five dots; 5-point star; cross; king's head with crown
Latin Locos (Folk Nation)	black and tan	6-point star; initials LL
Latin Lovers (Folk Nation)	red and yellow	Heart with wings; pitch-forks; staggered initials LL
Latin Souls (Folk Nation)	black and maroon	Cross with initials LS
Latin Youth (Folk Nation)	blue and white	6-point star; initials LYZ

Mafia Insane Vice Lord (People Nation)	black and gold, black and red	*see* Vice Lords
Maniac Latin Disciples (Folk Nation)	black and blue	Devil's head; crossed pitchforks; initials MLD or LD; heart with devil's horns and tail; backward swastika
Mickey Cobras (People Nation)	black and red	Cobra; initials MC; 5-point star
Orchestra Albany (Folk Nation)	brown and yellow	Initials OA
PR Stones (People Nation)	black and orange	5-point star; pyramid; words PR STONES
Ridgeway Lords (Folk Nation)	black and blue	6-point star; initials RL
Satan Disciples (Folk Nation)	black and yellow	6-point star, devil; pitchfork
Simon City Royals (Folk Nation)	black and blue	6-point star; Playboy bunny with bent ear; hat with crossed, double-barreled shotguns; initials SCR
Spanish Cobras (Folk Nation)	black and green	Coiled king cobra snake; initials SC
Spanish Gangster Disciples (Folk Nation)	black and light blue	Pitchforks; 6-point star; heart with horns
Spanish Lords (People Nation)	black and red	Crown; initials SL; heart with a cross
Spanish Vice Lords (People Nation)	black and gold, black and red	*see* Vice Lords

Two Sixers (Folk Nation)	black and tan	Playboy bunny with a fedora or cocked ear; set of tan and black dice showing two dots and six dots, or two dots and the numeral 6; initials TSN
Two Two Boys (Folk Nation)	black and blue	Two dice showing the numeral 2, or having two dots on each; crest or shield with two lions
Undertaker Vice Lords (People Nation)	black and gold, black and red	*see* Vice Lords
Unknown Vice Lords (People Nation)	black and gold, black and red	*see* Vice Lords
Vice Lords (People Nation)	black and gold, black and red	Crescent moon with 5-point star; top hat with cane; pyramid with crescent moon; martini glass; Playboy bunny head; pair of dice with the numerals 2 and 3; initials VL
Warlords (People Nation)	black and white	5-point star; initials WL

This 19" x 14" pastel painting was purchased by the author at a high-school auction raising money for the Humane Society. Note the gang symbols: a five-point star, five teeth on the hat, the dog jumping at a crescent moon, and the left-handed batter—all symbols of the Vice Lord Nation. This picture managed to get by school authorities.

This tee shirt is painted with Vice Lord symbols. Note the pyramid with an eye, the crescent moon with the five-point star, and the numeral 7. The number 7 inside the circle represents the Seven Acts, or prayers, of the Koran; the circle, which is 360°, signifies that black people once ruled the world and will rule again. Also notice the manner in which rival gang symbols are displayed: a broken six-point star and a broken, upside-down heart with a devil's tail and horn. This is meant to insult the Latin Disciples, their rival gang,

Gang Graffiti

Symbols and graffiti go hand in hand. Gangs write their symbols on schoolbooks, clothing, business cards (yes, there are business cards for gang members), and anywhere else a gang wants to make a statement. And of course, symbols are almost always found in gang graffiti, which is used to mark turf, display street names, intimidate other gangs, honor slain comrades, and let the world know that a gang exists. Graffiti may be written on walls, buses, trains, telephone poles, dumpsters, garages, street signs—anything that has a suitable surface.

Graffiti has been called "the gang's newspaper," and for good reason. It conveys messages to other gangs while promoting or

Black Gangster Disciples

Satan Disciples

Graffiti of the Folk Nation

Orchestra Albany

Maniac Latin Disciples

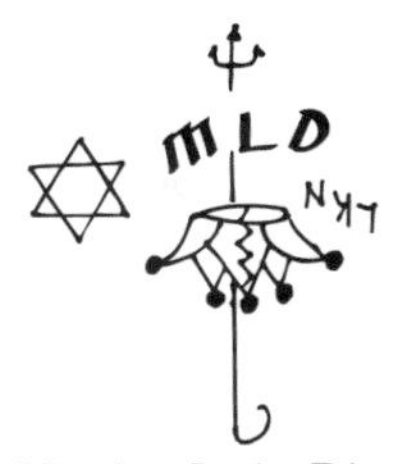

Maniac Latin Disciples (showing disrespect to the Latin Kings)

Simon City Royals

GRAFFITI OF THE PEOPLE NATION

Undertaker Vice Lords — *PR Stones* — *Mickey Cobras "All is Well"*

Future Stones — *Conservative Vice Lords* — *Latin Kings*

Insane Unknowns — *El Rukns*

glorifying one's own gang. It is purposely written in a way that is meant to confuse the general public. For example, Hispanic gang members will sometimes use Spanish, or a combination of English and Spanish, in their graffiti. Occasionally, they will draw letters in varying positions or use different style loops and serifs to make it even more difficult for the public to read.

When a neighborhood is marked with graffiti, it could be a site for serious trouble. Residents should be on the lookout for different types of graffiti walls. A Roll Call Wall, for example, contains the street names or monikers of different gang members of a particular set, hood, barrio, clique, or area. A RIP Wall lists the street names of gang members who have been killed in gang fights, drive-by shootings, and other types of violence. Graffiti on this wall will often contain a picture of a tombstone with the letters RIP (Rest In Peace). Graffiti found on a Justice Wall typically shows opposition to rival gangs, displaying their symbols upside down, broken in half, or otherwise distorted.

Defacing Gang Graffiti

Whether covering another gang's graffiti or displaying a rival's symbols in an offensive manner, defacing gang symbols is a way of letting everyone know who's been there, who's there now, and how they feel about rival gangs. The purposeful defacing of another gang's symbols is the equivalent of one person challenging another to a pistol duel. It cannot be ignored.

There are a number of ways gang members deface another gang's symbols:

- Painting or drawing rival symbols—such as a cane, staff, star, crown, heart, or cross—broken in half.
- Displaying rival gang symbols in an upside-down or inverted position, such as a pitchfork pointing downward.
- Painting or drawing one's own gang symbols directly over a rival gang's symbols. The new paint will usually have the colors of the gang that is doing the defacing.
- Writing a rival gang's name either upside down or backward.
- Crossing out letters that correspond to a rival gang's initials, usually with one's own gang colors.

This graffiti was found in Skokie, Illinois, in a library book about street gangs. It was drawn by a member of the Insane Satan Disciples. Notice how the lettering is deliberately written in a way that makes it almost unreadable to the untrained eye. Parents and educators should learn how to read gang graffiti, particularly the words and phrases. In this example, we see the words "Insane Satan Disciples," a six-point star, and a devil's head.

The graffiti on page 91 comes from the same library book, and was also written by a member of the Insane Satan Disciples. It is meant to insult members of any People gang. If you look carefully, you will notice the following:

1. The phrase at the top reads: "5 killer n go down ain't no sin, cause Satan will always win."

2. A five-point star, a symbol of the People Nation, is broken in half.

3. A pyramid, also a symbol of the People Nation, is displayed upside down with a crack down the middle.

4. A robed figure, which is a symbol of certain People gangs, is displayed upside down and broken in half.

5. A six-point star with devil's horns and tail (Folk symbols). Notice that the tail snares the pyramid, a People symbol.

6. The initials SD stand for Satan Disciples.

7. The gang's name, Insane Satan Disciples, is written in the lower left-hand corner.

Gang Graffiti Found in a Library Book

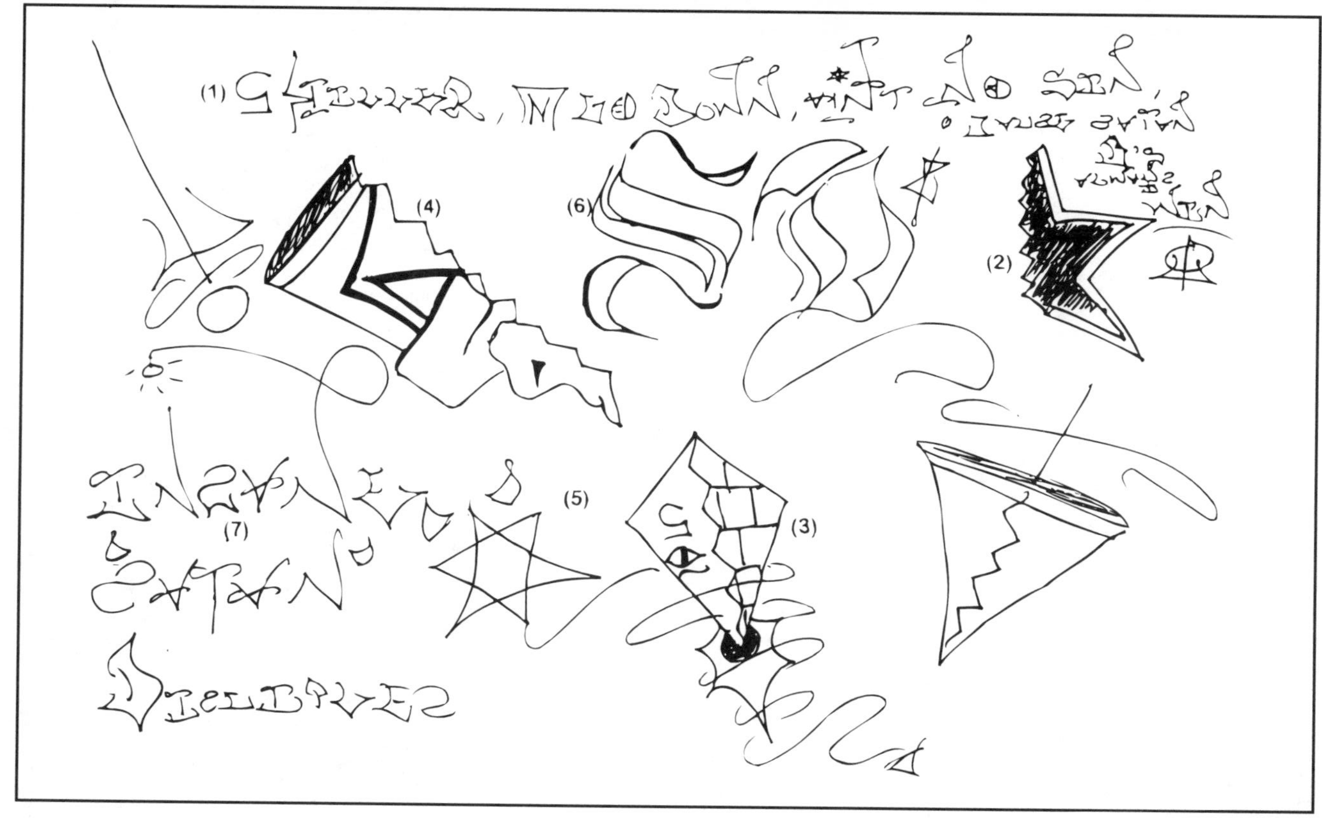

This is an example of a Roll Call/Justice Wall. Measuring approximately 9' x 10', it was found in an apartment in a town of fewer than 5000 residents. If you look closely, you will see that the monikers of members of the Latin Kings are listed. Symbols displayed here include 1) a king's head looking to the left and wearing a five-point crown, and 2) a second crown with five points and the numeral 5 (lower left-hand corner). Also, there are several defaced Folk symbols: 1) an upside-down, cracked heart with devil's horns, 2) a pitchfork pointing downward, dripping with blood, and 3) several upside-down pitchforks (to the right of the heart).

Graffiti displayed by the Maniac Latin Disciples. Note the heart with devil's horns and tail, the initials MLD inside the heart, the backward swastika, and the pitchforks pointing upward.

This Roll Call Wall was found on the side of a house in Chicago. It was probably written by the Latin Kings. Note the five-point crown with five dots, and the downward pitchfork next to the letter S (this shows disrespect to the Folk Nation). Underneath the crown is the moniker "Spanky" (notice how the letter "n" in Spanky is a downward pitchfork). Below that, on the brick, is the moniker "Capone." To the far left is another downward pitchfork and the words "Disciple Killer" written in fancy lettering.

This graffiti was left by two members of the Vice Lord Nation. Note the staff which runs through the names—a Vice Lord symbol.

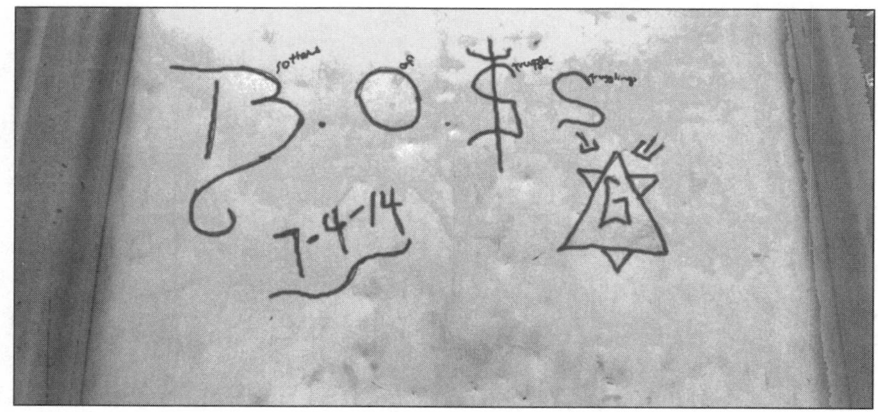

The graffiti above was found on a playground slide at a housing project near Chicago. BOSS stands for "Brothers of the Struggle Struggling." The numbers 7-4-14 correspond to the alphabet letters GDN, meaning Gangster Disciples Nation. For more information on the use of numbers in graffiti, see Appendix Two.

This is an example of graffiti written by the Latin Kings. Note the gang symbols: a crown with five points, five dots, and the initials LK. Also displayed are a broken six-point star (above the crown) and an upside-down pitchfork (attached to the letter K) to show disrespect to the Folk Nation.

Gang Jewelry

Jewelry is an important part of a gang member's wardrobe. The sale of gang-inspired jewelry is a fast-growing business targeting inner-city and suburban youths from coast to coast. But when trying to determine if a child is involved with a gang, keep in mind that some pieces of jewelry—the six-point star (Star of David) and the crescent moon with a single star, for example—indicate religious affiliation, not necessarily gang involvement.

Gang jewelry can be very revealing. Pendants shaped like Tec-9s (with protruding ammunition clips), crowns, pyramids, dollar signs, swastikas, and so on leave little doubt about gang involvement. And more specific emblems—six-point stars with the initials GD (Gangster Disciples), for example—signify specific gangs. Some of the jewelry is heavy, elaborate, and very expensive. Much, though, is ten karat, tinny, potato-chip thin, and made to look more expensive than it really is. Call it a lot of flash for a little cash. Many of the heavier pieces can be bought for between $60 and $150. However, sterling silver and gold-plated gang jewelry sell for between $2 and $8 each. These are available to even the youngest children, who generally can't afford the more expensive pieces.

While researching the article "Jewelry To Die For," published in the *Chicago Tribune,* 22 June 1993, reporters Robert Blau and David Jackson visited several jewelry stores in Chicago. They discovered that there is a market for gang jewelry—a big market. Teenagers would spread out hundreds or even thousands of dollars on the counter, in tens and twenties, no questions asked. Merchants reported having to count out the money for youths who were unable to do so themselves. Merchants are looking the other way when it comes to these big cash sales. "You're in a business to make money, and if I don't, somebody else will," one merchant said. "I don't got a choice."

Of course, they do have a choice. But without any community pressure to stop, they will continue with business as usual. The profits are just too good. For my own research, I went to seven different jewelry stores in the Chicago area, all of them independently owned. (I visited national chains as well, but none carried any gang jewelry.) Each time I entered a store with my camera, the merchants eyed me suspiciously. Time and again I was told to leave, and on one occasion, the store owner became so agitated at my presence with a camera that he threatened to call the police if I didn't leave immediately. Trying to bribe the merchants didn't help, either. In the middle of the afternoon, in the middle of the week, without any customers around, I couldn't even get a merchant to accept $30 to let me photograph his jewelry. The merchants knew exactly what they were selling, and they wanted no part of me.

The bottom line is this: it's not illegal to sell gang jewelry. Some jewelry merchants don't care whom they sell their jewelry to, or how their customers obtain the money to buy it. It doesn't matter if a hard-core gang member spreads out a thousand dollars, or an eight-year-old third grader comes in with $5 to spend. A sale is a sale. After all, jewelry doesn't kill people; people kill people, right? Only pressure from parents, educators, clergy, and civic leaders will convince these jewelry merchants that gang jewelry is unwelcome in their community. Remember, jewelry merchants have a constitutional right to sell this type of jewelry. But we as citizens have the constitutional right to let them know how we feel about it.

The gang jewelry displayed in this book represents only a small sample of what is available.

AFRICAN AMERICAN GANGS

African American gang jewelry comes in many shapes and styles. Pendants, rings, and earrings showing the six-point star are popular among Folks. Gangster Disciples often engrave the initials GD in the center of the six-point star, or they wear the Masonic symbol, also used in pendants and rings, for the letter G found in the design. Jewelry containing a Playboy bunny symbol with a bent ear represents a Folk affiliation, whereas a Playboy bunny symbol with a straight ear indicates membership with the People.

Other jewelry that is popular with the People gangs includes pendants and rings that show crescent moons, the five-point star, pyramids, Spanish crosses, the number 5, and dice.

Pendants, rings, and earrings shaped like Uzis, AK-47s, Mac-9s, Mac-10s, and other automatic guns are popular among all African American gangs. Gang jewelry isn't limited to just gang symbols, though. Some carry nationally known logos and characters, such as Mickey Mouse, Mercedes Benz, Fila, Gucci, Nike, and Adidas. Other designs found on gang jewelry include playing cards, a cannabis leaf, and the letter X (for Malcolm X). African American gangs refer to gold necklaces as "flats," "bones," "links," and "dukey ropes."

Male gang members will sometimes wear earrings with gang symbols in either the right or left ear to show their affiliation. It should be noted that in many parts of the country, the wearing of a single earring in the right ear denotes homosexuality. For this reason, many African American gang members will wear earrings in both ears. Female gang members tend to avoid large pendants or rings, but will wear earrings with gang symbols to show their affiliation.

Both male and female African American gang members sometimes wear friendship bracelets. A few years ago, these bracelets were made of a gummylike substance and were appropriately called "jelly bracelets." Today, they are generally hand-woven with gang colors.

These sterling silver pieces retail for about $2 each. The symbols are 1) a five-point star, worn by the People Nation, 2) a six-point star, worn by the Folk Nation, 3) dollar signs, which are popular among most gang members, 4) a crescent moon with a star, belonging to the Vice Lords, 5) a rounded crown, exclusive to the Latin Kings and other People Nation gangs, and 6) a revolver, popular among most gang members.

These sterling silver pieces retail for $4 to $5 each. The quarter shows the scale. They are 1) a rounded crown, worn by the Latin Kings (the words KING is spelled out at the bottom), 2) a Tec-9, popular among many gangs, 3) a five-point crown, belonging exclusively to the Latin Kings and other People Nation gangs, 4) a Masonic symbol, which has been adopted by the Gangster Disciples for the letter G in the center, and 5) a five-point star, used by the People Nation.

Hispanic gangs

Hispanic gangs also purchase gold and silver gang jewelry in a variety of shapes. Gold chains are popular, and most gang members wear a cross. Custom gold pendants that spell out the wearer's name, or a boyfriend's or girlfriend's name, are also common. Latin Kings sometimes wear crosses that are hand-woven with gang colors, but they are more likely to wear jewelry having a crown in the design. Particularly popular is the Claddagh, an Irish friendship ring, which has a crown in its center.

The handwoven Crucifix, made with gang colors, is popular among Hispanic Folk gangs, although some African American Folk gangs wear them as well.

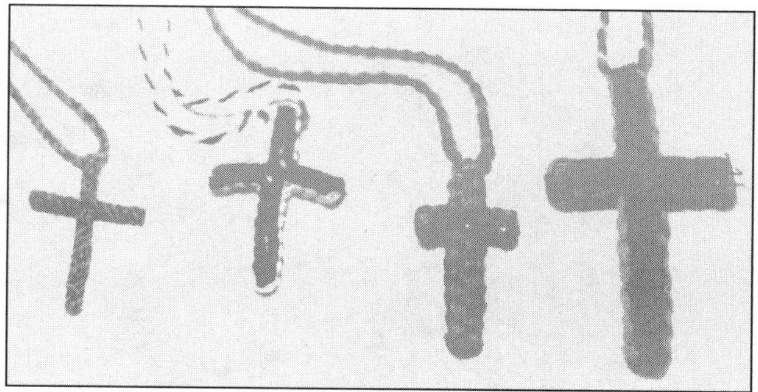

SKINHEAD GANGS

Parents and educators should be on the lookout for jewelry promoting Skinhead, neo-Nazi, and white supremacist ideology. Some of this jewelry may include authentic Nazi emblems, buttons, and lapel pins from the 1930s and 1940s. Iron Crosses, double lightning bolts (SS insignia), skulls (death heads), swastikas, and other paraphernalia can be found in antique stores, at regional gun shows, and among private collectors. Because authentic Nazi jewelry fetches a high price, Skinheads proudly wear these pieces on their clothing, particularly on the jacket.

Nazi armband with swastika

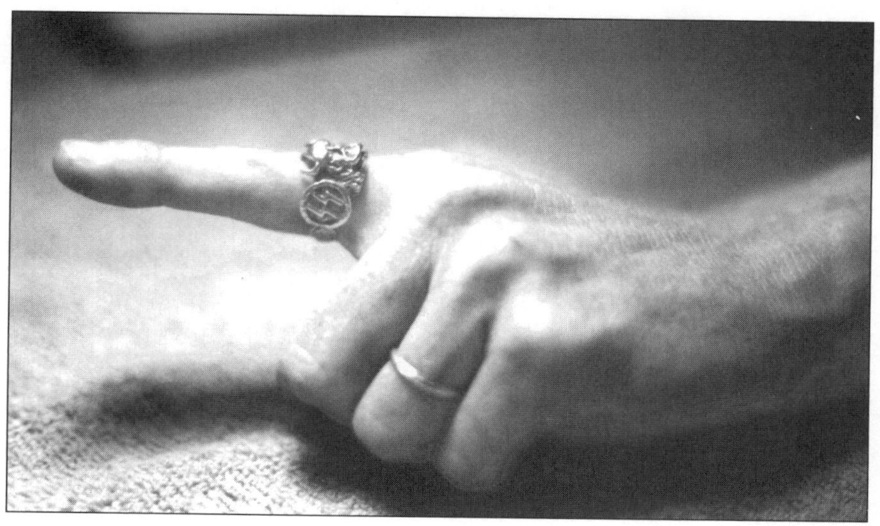

Sterling silver ring with Viking head and SS lightning bolts.

The famous "death head" emblem, worn by the Nazi death squads.

Nazi lapel pins

Iron Crosses

Chapter 9

SPORTS TEAM CLOTHING

Sports team apparel is an important indicator of gang involvement. An African American, Hispanic, or Caucasian gang member will wear sports team clothing if the team colors correspond to their gang colors, or if the team logo looks like (or can be altered to look like) one of their gang symbols. But remember, Starter jackets, baseball caps, and other sports apparel are frequently worn by non-gang individuals, too. Gangs occasionally mistake people in certain sports clothing for rival gang members, leading to harassment and sometimes violence. Furthermore, because Starter jackets in particular can be very expensive, gang members have been known to confront an individual to steal his or her jacket. Either way, merely wearing a sports team Starter jacket places a youth in danger.

It's safe to assume that professional sports teams would rather not have their team colors or logos adopted by gangs. Nevertheless, retailers, licensing distributors, and marketing executives have been quick to cash in on the gang fad, and some have altered their sports team apparel to suit the needs of gangs. For example, silver and black, colors belonging to the L.A. Kings and Oakland Raiders, are very popular among Folk gangs. (Folks often wear these colors in addition to their specific gang colors.) Now, White Sox clothing, which was traditionally white and black, is available in black and silver as well. Retailers actually *created* a whole new color combination for the Chicago White Sox, simply to take advantage of the gang market. Some have gone so far as to have kids in their ads pose with gang colors, with their caps tilted to one side.

Parents must be aware of what their children are wearing outside the home. If your child is wearing a Los Angeles Kings Starter jacket, ask him or her who the Los Angeles Kings are. Ask if he or she has ever watched the team play. If the answer is "no," you may have a problem. If you and your child live in a high-gang area, the safest best is to *wear neutral clothing*.

The following list describes gangs that have adopted specific sports clothing, and shows how the team colors and logos are used. Remember, with thousands of gangs nationwide it is best to check with local law enforcement officials to find out which gangs have adopted which sports teams in your area.

Sports Apparel Worn by Gangs Affiliated with the Folk and People Nations

Baseball

Team	Gang	Explanation
Anaheim Angels	Ambrose	This gang uses the logo letter A unaltered.
Atlanta Braves	People Nation	Some gangs affiliated with the People Nation use the logo initial A to mean "Almighty."
Boston Red Sox	Black Disciples	The Black Disciples sometimes add a letter D after the Red Sox logo (the letter B) to spell out their initials.
Chicago Cubs	Crips, Spanish Cobras	The Cubs logo is the letter C. Crips will color the letter blue. Spanish Cobras sometimes place an S to the left of the C to spell out their initials.
Chicago White Sox	Folk Nation, Satan Disciples	The letter O on the SOX logo has six points, which Folks use to represent the 6-point star. Satan Disciples color the letter S on the logo yellow.
Cincinnati Reds	4 Corner Hustlers	The C logo is altered by placing the numeral 4 to the left of the C, and the letter H inside of it.

Detroit Tigers	Disciples, Gangster Disciples	The team colors correspond to the gang colors, black and blue. Gangster Disciples sometimes place the letter G to the left of the Tigers logo (the Roman letter D). Other Disciples place a letter N to the right of the D, spelling the initials for Disciple Nation.
Houston Astros	4 Corner Hustlers	The gang uses the team logo unaltered: the letter H in a 5-point star.
Kansas City Royals	Folk Nation, Simon City Royals	Some gangs affiliated with the Folk Nation wear Royals apparel for the team colors, black and blue. Simon City Royals wear it for the name ROYALS on the logo.
LA Dodgers	Disciples, Gangster Disciples	Disciples use the Dodgers colors, black and blue, and their logo, the letter D. Gangster Disciples sometimes add the letter G to the left side of the D; other Disciple gangs will place the letter N to the right of the letter D, spelling the initials for Disciple Nation.
Minnesota Twins	Maniac Latin Disciples	Maniac Latin Disciples use the Twins logo, the letter M. They sometimes add the letters L and D to the right of the M, spelling out the gang's initials.
NY Yankees	Gangster Disciples	Gangster Disciples wear Yankees apparel for the team colors, black and blue.

Oakland Athletics (also known as the Oakland A's)	Ambrose, Orchestra Albany	Both gangs wear Oakland A's apparel for the logo letter A. Orchestra Albany members, however, sometimes add an O before the A, spelling out their gang's initials.
Philadelphia Phillies	People Nation	Some gangs affiliated with the People Nation wear Phillies apparel for the team logo, the letter P.
Pittsburgh Pirates	Spanish Lords, Vice Lords	These gangs sometimes wear Pirates apparel for the team logo, the letter P (which they use to represent the People Nation), and the team colors, black and gold.
St. Louis Cardinals	Bloods, Spanish Vice Lords	Both gangs wear Cardinals apparel for the team color, red.
Texas Rangers	People Nation	People Nation gangs wear Rangers apparel for the letter T in the logo, which looks like a downward pitchfork. (By displaying a downward pitchfork, People gangs show disrespect to Folk gangs).

Basketball

Team	**Gang**	**Explanation**
Boston Celtics	Spanish Cobras	Spanish Cobras wear Celtics apparel for the team colors, black and green.
Charlotte Hornets	4 Corner Hustlers, Crips, Gangster Disciples	The 4 Corner Hustlers sometimes place a numeral 4 to the left of the Hornet logo (the letters C and H). Crips wear Hornets apparel for the letter C in the logo. Gangster Disciples wear it for the hornet itself: the hornet's right hand has four fingers pointing downward, which the gang uses to show disrespect to the 4 Corner Hustlers.
Chicago Bulls	Vice Lords, Micky Cobras, Bloods, Maniac Latin Disciples	Both the Vice Lords and the Mickey Cobras wear Bulls apparel for the team colors, black and red. Bloods wear it for the color red. Maniac Latin Disciples have adopted this team because of the horns on the bull logo.
Orlando Magic	Folk Nation	Some Folk gangs wear Orlando Magic apparel for the colors, black and blue, and for the 5-point star (which replaces the letter A in the "Magic" logo). Folks will draw a crack in the 5-point star to show disrespect for the People Nation.
Phoenix Suns	Black Peace Stone Nation	This gang wears Suns apparel for the letters P and S found in the logo.

FOOTBALL

TEAM	**GANG**	**EXPLANATION**
Dallas Cowboys	People Nation	Some gangs affiliated with the People Nation wear Cowboys apparel for the 5-point star logo.
Denver Broncos	Black Disciples	Black Disciples use the logo letters DB, which spell out their gang's initials backward.
Detroit Lions	Folk Nation	Some gangs affiliated with the Folk Nation wear Lions apparel for the team colors, black and blue.
Kansas City Chiefs	Bloods	Bloods wear this team's apparel for the team color, red.
New Orleans Saints	Vice Lords	Vice Lords wear Saints apparel for the team colors, black and gold.
New York Giants	Crips	Crips wear Giants apparel for the team color, blue.
Oakland Raiders	Folk Nation, Crips	Crips and other gangs affiliated with the Folk Nation wear Raiders apparel for the team colors, black and silver, and the logo, a patch covering the right eye of the pirate (Folk gangs display on the right).

Hockey

Team	Gang	Explanation
Chicago Black Hawks	People Nation	Certain gangs affiliated with the People Nation wear Black Hawks apparel for the team colors, black and red, and the logo: a Native American wearing a headdress, with a downward pitchfork painted above his eye (the downward pitchfork shows disrespect to the Folk Nation).
Dallas North Stars (formerly the Minnesota North Stars)	People Nation	Gangs affiliated with the People Nation wear Dallas Stars apparel for the team logo, the 5-point star.
L.A. Kings (formerly the Los Angeles Kings)	Latin Kings, Folk Nation	Latin Kings wear the L.A. Kings apparel for the crown found in the team logo. Gang members sometimes black out the letters L and A to show just the word "Kings." Some Folk gangs wear this apparel for the team colors, black and silver.

Collegiate Teams

Team	Gang	Explanation
Duke University	Folk Nation	Some Folk Nation gangs wear Duke sports apparel for the team logo, the devil, and the color blue. Folks use the word DUKE to mean Disciples Utilizing Knowledge Everywhere.
University of Illinois	Folk Nation	Some Folk gangs wear this apparel for the logo initials I and U, which overlap into the shape of a pitchfork.
University of Indiana	Folk Nation	Some Folk gangs wear this sports apparel for the initials I and U, which overlap into the shape of a pitchfork.
Georgetown Hoyas	Gangster Disciples	Gangster Disciples wear this sports apparel for the team colors, black and blue, and the logo: a dog collar with six spikes, a letter G on the dog's cap, and the cap tilted to the right. They will sometimes add the letter D to the right of the G to spell out their gang's initials.
Georgia Tech	Gangster Disciples	Gangster Disciples wear Georgia Tech sports apparel for the logo initial G. They sometimes add a letter D to the right of the G, spelling out their gang's initials.
University of Miami Hurricanes	Future Stones, PR Stones	These gangs wear Hurricanes apparel for the team color, orange.

University of Michigan	Maniac Latin Disciples	Maniac Latin Disciples wear Michigan sports apparel for the logo letter M. They sometimes add the letters L and D to the right of the M, spelling out their gang's initials.
North Carolina Tar Heels	Folk Nation	Certain gangs affiliated with the Folk Nation wear this team's apparel for the colors, black and blue.
UNLV	Vice Lords, Bloods	Vice Lords wear this sports apparel for the colors black and red, and the initials UNLV (which they use to stand for Vice Lords Nation United, written backward). Bloods wear this apparel for the color red.

MISCELLANEOUS SPORTS APPAREL

NAME	GANG	EXPLANATION
Converse All Star Shoes	People Nation	Some People gangs wear Converse All Star shoes for the 5-point star located on the side. Many color the star with their gang colors.
Nike	Folk Nation	Some Folk gangs wear Nike apparel for the colors, blue and black.
Starter	People Nation, Folk Nation	People Nation gangs wear Starter apparel for the logo, the 5-point star. Folk Nation gangs will also wear Starter apparel, but will crack the star to show disrespect for the People.

Chapter 10

LANGUAGE AND HAND SIGNS

GANG LANGUAGE

Gangs use their own language to communicate with one another. African American and Hispanic gang members in particular use a variety of terms, phrases, and words to greet each other, identify themselves, and show disrespect to rival gang members. Parents and educators should familiarize themselves with gang terms and listen for children using any of the phrases. If they even jokingly use these words or phrases in public, and a gang member overhears, it could bring about a dangerous situation.

Carefully review the glossary at the end of this book. Keep in mind that young people who are not affiliated with gangs use these words and phrases in everyday conversation, too.

The following are specific African American gang words, initials, and slang that make up their own special gang language.

Crips

Crips greet each other with the word "cuzz," which is the abbreviated form of "cousin." They also call each other "BK," which stands for Blood Killer. To put down their rival gang, Crips avoid using words that begin with the letter B. For example, a Crip would avoid the common street phrase, "What it be like?" and instead say, "What it cee like?" Crips also insult Bloods by calling them "slobs." When a Crip calls a Blood a slob, it is almost a direct challenge for a fight.

Bloods

Bloods greet each other using the word "Blood" (or "Piru," if they are from the Compton area where Pirus originated). Bloods avoid using words that begin with the letter C. To put down Crips, and to "dis" them directly, Bloods call Crips "crabs" or "E-Rickette."

Folks

Members of the Folk Nation use the motto All is One to greet one another and to determine the affiliation of unknown gang members who enter their neighborhood. A gang member who wants to insult a Vice Lord will call him or her a "Vicky Lou" or a "hook."

People

Members of the People Nation use the motto All is Well to greet one another and determine gang affiliation. Gang members will insult Disciples by calling them "donuts."

Hispanic Gangs

Many Hispanic gang members will use Spanish, or a combination of English and Spanish, in their conversations with one another. One of the more popular words that Hispanic gangs use is *Ese* (pronounced like the letters SA). The word literally means "man," "dude," "vato," or "gang member," and is scattered throughout Hispanic gang conversation.

Some Hispanic gang members will use Spanish exclusively when in the presence of other non-Spanish speaking gangs or individuals.

Hand Signs

Gang members from the major African American and Hispanic groups described in this book use hand signs to communicate. Fingers and hands are positioned to show letters, numbers, and words. A hand sign may be one singular movement, or a series of movements using one or both hands. When one gang member gives a hand sign to another, it is called "flagging" or "throwing." Members of the Folk Nation will throw their signs from the right side, and the People Nation will throw theirs from the left.

Gangs have learned to exploit the American Sign Language (ASL) alphabet and numerals, using these signs to indicate gang affiliation. For example, a member of the Crips will sign the letter "C" followed by a numeral to show which neighborhood or street he or she comes from. Parents and educators of hearing-impaired children should be aware of the dangers these children might face when using ASL outside of the home or school. More than one deaf person in this country has been mistaken for a gang member, by both actual gang members and police, when seen using ASL. In 1995, a deaf man in Minneapolis was badly beaten on a city bus when a gang mistook

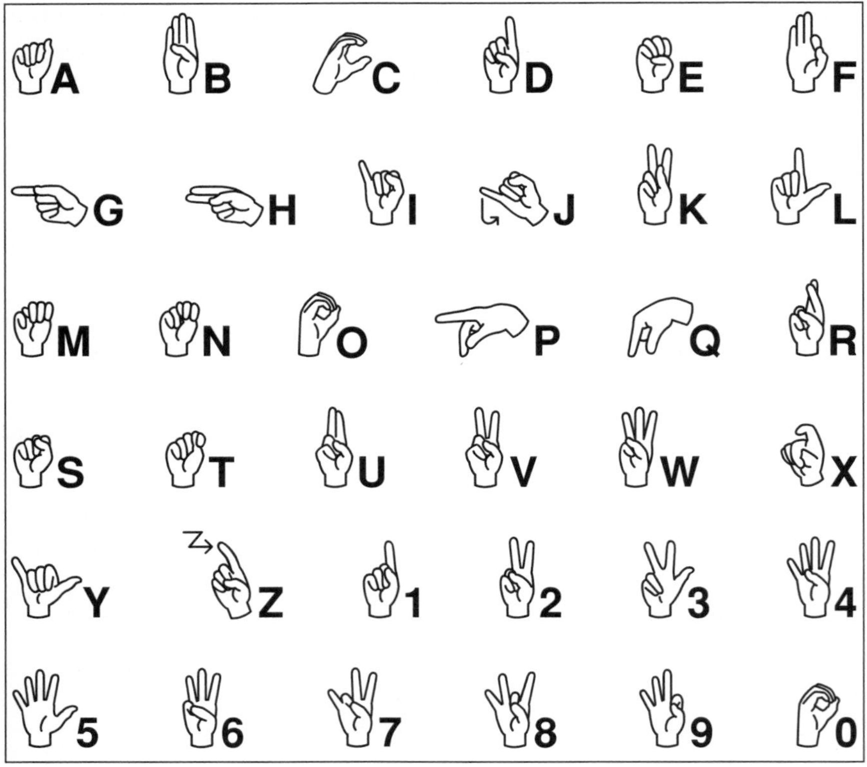

American Sign Language alphabet and numbers

his sign language for rival gang signs. He lost an eye in the incident. Similar attacks have taken place across the country.

There are thousands of gangs throughout the United States, and gang hand signs are inevitably duplicated. For example, gang members often use ASL to spell out their gang's initials. There is a gang in Cleveland, Ohio, called the Hilltop Posse, and one in Newark, New Jersey, called Hangman Posse. Both gangs have the initials HP, and both may use the same hand signs to spell out their initials.

Parents and educators should be able to recognize at least a few of the different hand signs that gangs use. Parents should observe how their children behave around their friends both at home and in the community. Teachers who see students flash gang signs need to take immediate action in accordance with school guidelines. Children should never jokingly flash gang signs. Gang members take a serious view of this behavior and tend to react harshly.

There are a number of ways gang members give one another a sign, and each has a significant meaning. Gang members will flash or throw their own signals to one another to declare unity or to determine the gang affiliation of an unknown gang member. A member will also "throw down" a gang sign as a warning or show of disrespect to another gang. That is, he or she will throw a rival gang member's hand sign upside down or with a downward motion. A rival gang member will view this as a direct challenge.

A gang member will occasionally flash a false gang sign to a rival gang member. This is called "false flagging." The false sign is the rival gang member's sign. It is meant to trick a possible rival into revealing his or her gang affiliation. If the rival gang member, thinking that he or she is acknowledging a fellow gang member, flashes back this sign, it may lead to violence. For example, some Vice Lords may want to retaliate against the Imperial Gangsters for violating their turf. The Vice Lord members travel into Imperial Gangster territory and flash the Imperial Gangster sign to an individual. The individual nods and returns the sign in acknowledgment. That individual is now an instant target for the Vice Lords.

The following pages show just a few of the different hand signs that Crips, Bloods, Folks, and People use. Bear in mind that many of the thousands of gangs throughout the United States have their own unique hand signs. This is only a very small sample, but it should give you an idea of what to look for.

Crip Hand Signs

Harlem Crips

Playboy Gangster Crips

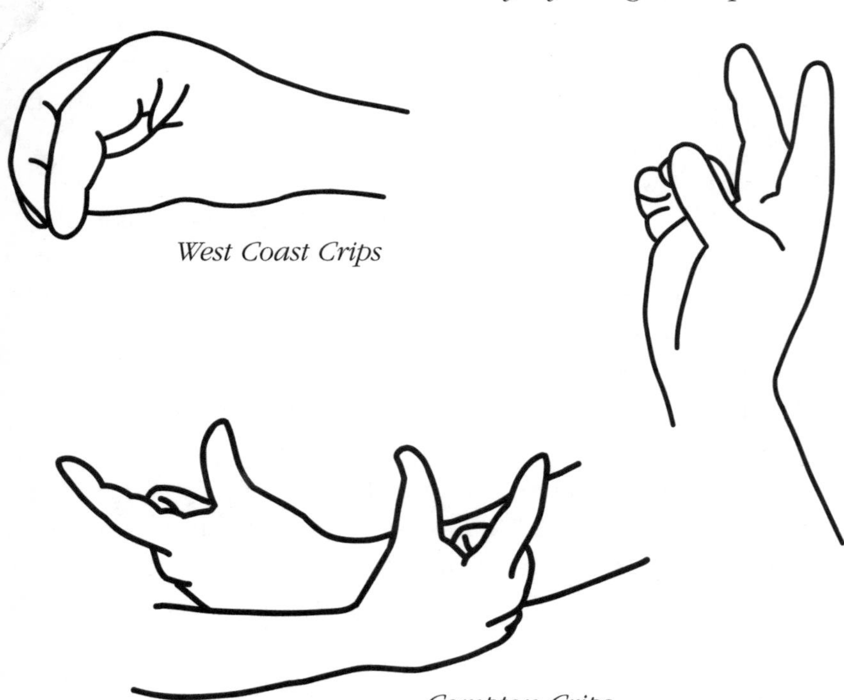

West Coast Crips

Compton Crips

Blood Hand Signs

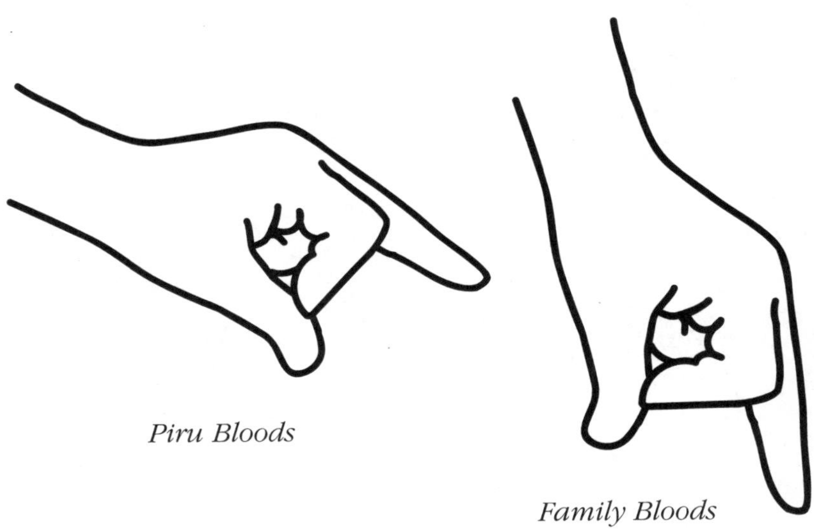

Piru Bloods

Family Bloods

Brim Bloods

Neighborhood Bloods

Folk Hand Signs

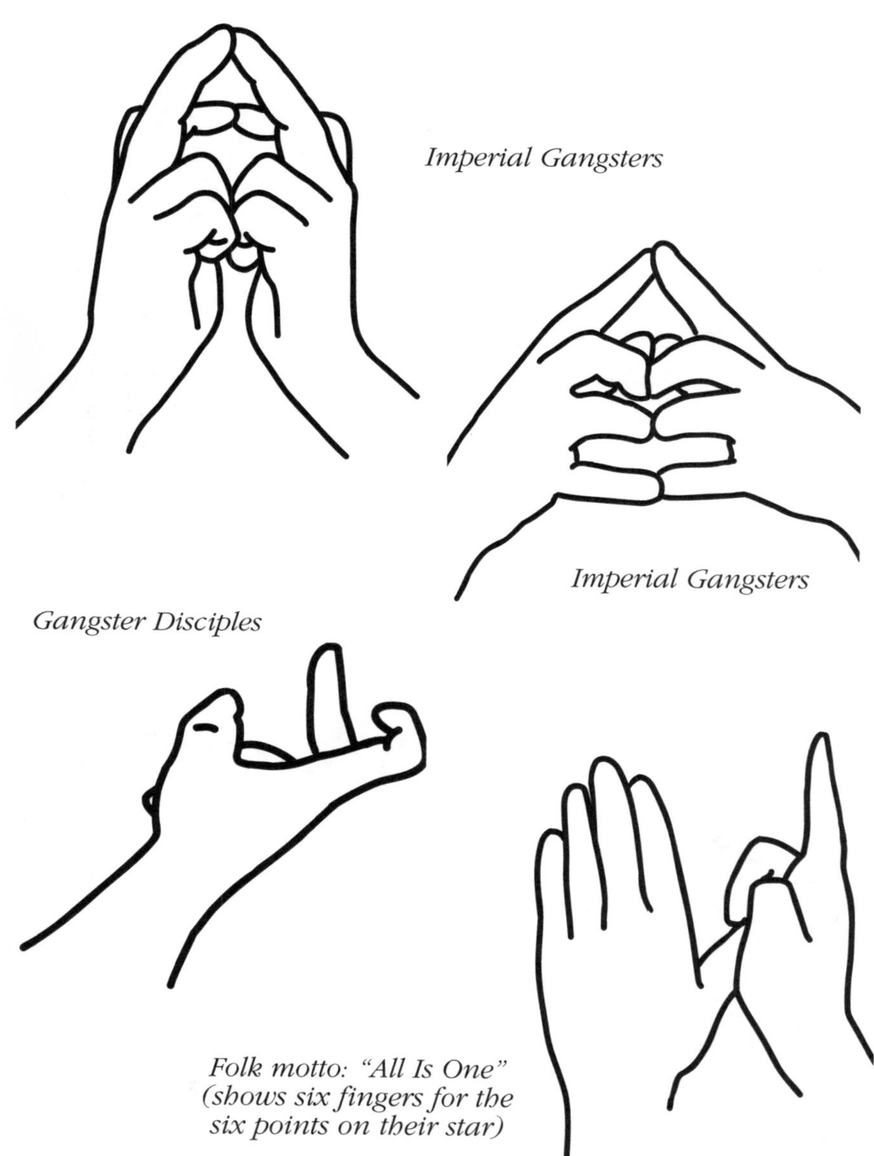

Imperial Gangsters

Imperial Gangsters

Gangster Disciples

Folk motto: "All Is One" (shows six fingers for the six points on their star)

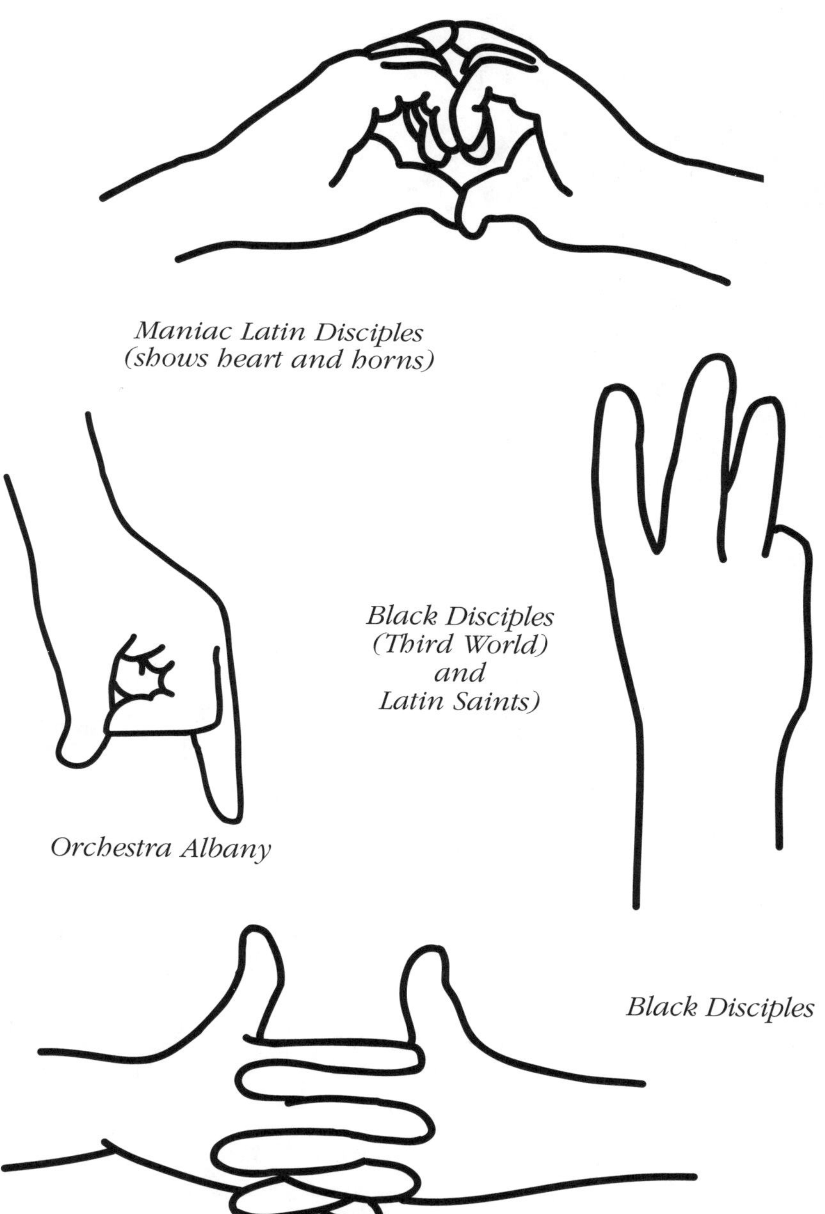

Maniac Latin Disciples (shows heart and horns)

Orchestra Albany

Black Disciples (Third World) and Latin Saints)

Black Disciples

People Hand Signs

Five-point star
(People Nation symbol)

Latin Kings

Latin Kings

Insane Unknowns

Vice Lords (showing the initials VL)

Part Four

Steering Kids Away From Gangs

Chapter 11

COMMUNITY RESPONSE

This book will help parents and professionals identify the danger signs of gangs and gang activity. But this is really only a starting point. Steering kids away from gangs is a long, tough process. There is no magic solution. Some children can be moved in the right direction at an early age. But parents must get involved. There is no way around it. Society cannot afford to wait for the government to step in and solve the gang problem. When parents can look to friends, family, schools, law enforcement, churches, and community programs for help, the odds are more in their favor. And it helps them to know they are not alone.

Law Enforcement

When it comes to dealing with gangs, perhaps no single resource is as knowledgeable, or as motivated, as local and state police and county sheriff's departments. Law enforcement agencies, large and small, face gangs and gang activity daily. Many have specialized gang units.

But law enforcement officials can only do so much. Parents and educators need to share their own expertise. There must be a dialogue between law enforcement officials and citizens, educators, and parents. Police should be invited to visit schools, patrol neighborhoods, and educate youths about the dangers of gangs and gang life.

Departments across the country are taking a proactive approach in dealing with the menace of gangs. The following is a list of suggestions for law enforcement officials. Many of these programs have been used in different parts of the country with varying degrees of success.

• **Make gang identification materials, such as handouts and resource guides, available to the public.** Information should be written in English and translated into other languages used in the community, and it should be available at the front desk in every police department.

Of the suburban Chicago police departments I visited while researching this book (I posed as a concerned parent looking for information on gangs), only one in nine gave me a written handout to take home. I suspect this average would hold nationwide. The other department personnel were cordial, inviting me to speak to an officer on duty or suggesting that I return in the evening to talk with a gang officer (gang officers usually work in the evenings). For parents who suspect their son or daughter might be involved with a gang, returning to the police station for that conversation may simply be too daunting. Fear, or the desire to remain anonymous, might keep concerned parents away.

• **Produce video tapes about gang prevention and intervention, making them available to parents and educators for viewing at police stations, schools, or homes on a rental basis.** Parents who take a video tape home could invite other parents in the neighborhood to view it as well, or space at the local police station might be used for private viewing. (Yes, I know, space may be at a premium.) Literature could be produced to supplement the video.

• **Confiscate gang items from gang members.** The suburban town of Mundelein, Illinois, has already instituted this zero tolerance approach to the gang problem. Any youth arrested for gang activity is immediately searched, and all gang jewelry, hats with gang symbols, and other gang-related items found on his or her person are confiscated. The parents are notified and invited to come down to the police station to reclaim their child's gang items, but according to the police chief, no parent has yet acted on the offer, nor has any complained.

Before embarking on this type of policy, however, it may be wise to contact the city attorney and check municipal and state laws.

• **Advertise warnings about gangs.** No kidding! Tell parents about gangs, what to look for, and what resources are available. You'd be surprised what one well-placed article or series of articles in the local newspaper can do. Not only does it demystify gang culture, it also shows that help is available. Reprints of the article can then be sent to schools and given to parents as handouts.

Law enforcement officials have an obligation not only to protect citizens from gang activity, but also to take a proactive stance in educating the public about the dangers of gangs. The public also has a responsibility to report all gang activity to law enforcement officials. If left unchecked and unreported, gang activity will grow.

Youth Centers

Youth centers are a valuable resource in combating gang activity and its influence. They provide alternatives for gang members and other youths at risk by creating an opportunity for them to develop new skills, learn how to work with others, and build badly needed self-esteem. Youth centers are generally staffed by volunteers from the community, including parents, teachers, college students, paid professionals, and even former gang members.

The following are programs that some youth centers provide for youths and their families:

Employment and Job-Seeking Skills

Youths at risk need financial alternatives to the gang's methods of generating income. Many of them have never filled out a job application or had a job interview. Several good instructional programs on the market teach these skills. Two excellent resources are:

Government:

United States Department of Labor
Employment and Training Administration
Washington, D.C. 20210

Private:

Life Skills Education
226 Libbey Parkway
Weymouth, MA 02189
1-800-783-6743

Both offer low-cost pamphlets with instructions on such areas as résumé and cover letter writing, how to fill out a job application, and preparing for a job interview.

Youth centers on a tight budget can create their own pre-employment programs by using actual job applications and conducting mock interviews. They can even provide job listings and newspaper want ads, or act as liaisons to local businesses by providing a pool of prescreened adolescents who are interested in employment.

Counseling and Support Services

As studies over the years have shown, dysfunctional families have a much higher percentage of children who join gangs. These families, and many others, have been torn apart by gangs and gang activity. Counseling can help families communicate with one another and begin the healing process.

Youth centers could facilitate a number of family and individual counseling programs. The following have been offered by various youth centers around the nation:

- Gang mediation and awareness programs
- Prenatal counseling
- Parent-effectiveness training
- Anger-management classes

Recreation

Cheap, fun activities not only help kids build self-esteem, but also teach them communication skills that are occasionally transferred back to the neighborhood. A youth center could provide an activity center on its premises. Kids could join for a nominal fee—say, $5 or so—and enjoy the use of equipment like Ping Pong tables, a big screen TV, air hockey or pool tables, and a jukebox. Membership fees could be used to obtain new recreation equipment or maintain current equipment.

Youth centers can work with park districts and other city recreational programs to offer some of the following activities:

- Basketball/softball leagues
- Movie nights
- Athletic contests
- Amusement park excursions
- Bowling nights

Fees may be charged to cover ticket and travel expenses, but kids from lower-income families should also be allowed to participate at little or no cost. Some of the fees could be underwritten by local businesses or the city.

Communities that have gang problems but do not have a youth center should consider establishing one. A youth center would serve as a neutral zone for kids wanting to get away from dangerous neighborhoods and the gang environment. Staff should develop a zero tolerance policy toward any kind of gang activity within the youth center itself, but be sensitive to youths checking out the program for the first time. If the center turns away a kid because he or she is wearing gang colors, the center may lose the kid for good.

Of course, a youth center is affected by the financial climate of its community. Programs and activities are only as good as the financial funding that backs them. In my own community, the youth center is a converted fire station. Someone had the foresight to save the building from the wrecking ball, providing a safe haven for at-risk youths while conserving the community's limited financial resources.

Graffiti Removal

Graffiti removal programs, which have been launched in different communities nationwide, have great merit. Removing graffiti from buildings and other structures sends a message to gangs that they are not welcome. It also becomes a nuisance to gangs who use graffiti to claim turf, show disrespect to rival gangs, and communicate warnings. Graffiti removal is important because graffiti walls are critical to gang communication.

Neighborhood organizations can work with schools and local law enforcement officials to establish a network of graffiti removal projects. These projects could involve the perpetrators themselves (if they are caught) or other teenage offenders who are sentenced to perform community service. It is important to contact local law enforcement officials before beginning a graffiti removal project. They may want to photograph the graffiti to identify which gangs are in the area and document the extent of their activity. Also, law enforcement officials may need to protect graffiti removers from gang retaliation. Gangs are very protective of their graffiti, and for safety's sake, graffiti should never be removed by an individual working alone.

Tattoo Removal

For the last two years, a hospital in the Chicago area has offered low-cost tattoo removal and counseling ($25) for gang and ex-gang members. Staffed by doctors and nurses who volunteer their time, the program offers a method of tattoo removal that is both fast and easy, while providing important support to those who are leaving or have left the gang lifestyle. Several other cities have similar programs.

Neighborhood Organizations

Unfortunately, police patrols will not completely curb gang activity. Police sometimes arrive "after the fact": after the drive-by shooting occurred, after the mugging went down, after the drugs were sold. Neighbors must continue to band together and work with law enforcement officials to help eradicate gangs and gang activity. Some specific things a neighborhood association and its members can do are:

- **Report all gang activity and crimes.** It sounds simple, but many people are afraid to dial 911 when they see a crime in progress for fear of gang retaliation. Most police departments will request to meet the complainant in person, but you can inform the police dispatcher that you don't want to be seen. The dispatcher still has a duty to send a squad car to the area.

• **Organize a neighborhood watch.** Keep an eye out for suspicious activity and pay attention to the comings and goings of people and cars.

• **Be a visible presence.** Gangs tend to avoid neighborhoods where they see citizens walking their dogs, planting flowers, playing with their children, and doing other outdoor activities.

• **Work with law enforcement officials to help eradicate known gang houses.** Neighbors can take turns watching a gang house, noting descriptions of gang members, writing down license plate numbers, and videotaping or photographing gang activity. Caution: Don't risk your own safety to get these pictures. Take them discreetly, possibly from a window. Once this information is turned over to law enforcement officials, communities can pressure the landlord or owner of the house to have the current tenants (gang members) evicted. This effectively puts the landlord or property owner "on notice" that the neighborhood will not tolerate the renting of property to gang members or their associates.

Communities can take further steps against owners who are unwilling to involve themselves in the management of their property. Many cities are enacting property and civil abatement laws to motivate property owners to clean up their acts. Owners who allow their property to become a public nuisance may be fined or jailed, and they may even lose their property. Neighborhood organizations should inquire with local law enforcement officials and city prosecutors for more information on this legal maneuver.

• **Organize.** By far the most important thing a neighborhood can do is organize. Neighbors who act alone may find themselves the target of gangs. There is strength in numbers. Gangs know this and have used this tactic effectively. Now is the time for neighborhoods to do the same.

CHURCHES

One of the best resources parents can turn to is the church. Many churches throughout the United States have developed anti-gang programs that offer gang members and at-risk youths a number of services to help build self-esteem and provide alternatives to gang activity. Just like youth centers, churches can be staffed by college students, ex-gang members, parishioners, and other volunteers. Programs can also parallel those of youth centers, offering such activities as parenting classes, rap sessions, after-school tutoring, drug and alcohol prevention programs, and support groups. The added components of spiritual growth and discipline are very important as well. Some gang members will find that the spiritual laws of the Scripture leave no room for gang values.

Some churches have combined resources and formed coalitions to help combat the gang problem. Others have even gone so far as to offer a safe haven for families whose children are trying to leave a gang, but fear retribution and need to relocate to protect themselves. Unfortunately, these programs are few and far between. There are simply not enough churches willing to take the risk.

Look for a local church that offers a gang outreach program. Even if your child refuses to participate, the church can still provide support and assistance to you.

Chapter 12

SCHOOL RESPONSE

Many schools across the nation are developing a zero tolerance approach to gangs and gang activity. Many dress codes now include a ban on sports team Starter jackets, gang jewelry, and gang colors. Students' activities during lunch hours and before and after school are also closely monitored. Some schools offer students an after-school curriculum as an alternative to gang involvement. To the dismay of many parents, teachers, and school administrators, however, after-school programs are being eliminated nationwide because of budget restraints. It's a no-win situation. Communities cry out that society needs to combat gangs, yet those same communities defeat themselves by voting against tax increases for school budgets. We can't have it both ways.

The process of educating kids about gangs should start at an early age, particularly when kids live in a high-risk area, and there are numerous measures a school can take to combat gang activity. Recognition that a student is involved with a gang, or is seriously considering it, is the first step. The next step is to divert the student. The following measures have been used successfully by schools throughout the nation:

• **Continue to monitor current fashions and ban gang apparel,** particularly, altered sports team Starter jackets, gang jewelry, obvious gang color combinations, and gang buttons or patches. Teachers and administrators should not overreact, however.

Some gang apparel corresponds to trends in mainstream fashion. Be careful not to trample a child's constitutional rights. Rather, note specific emblems, added designs, symbols, lettering, and the manner in which certain clothing is worn. (See Part Three for information on gang identifiers.)

Some schools have addressed the problem of gang clothing by requiring students to follow dress codes. Carri Karuhn wrote a special feature article on this subject for the *Chicago Tribune* titled "Codes Help Pupils Dress for Success" (26 September 1996). Karuhn reports that in 1996, Chicago Unit District 300 adopted a specific clothing policy. Students at Carpentersville Middle School now wear either white or navy blue tops, with bottoms that are either navy blue or tan. Shoes must be a solid color with matching laces. No insignia or logos are permitted. According to school officials, a few parents were displeased with the policy at first, citing a possible violation of their children's First Amendment rights as well as the cost and inconvenience of having to purchase new clothes. The majority of parents, however, now favor the dress code policy. They no longer worry that gang bangers will cause problems over their children's clothing at school, and their children no longer pester them to buy the latest fashions. Karuhn also reports that the students themselves support the dress code policy. Many of the youngsters say it makes them look "nicer" as a whole. One student reports that he can concentrate more on his schoolwork and less on his clothes. A teacher claims that kids who can't afford expensive, trendy clothes appear more self-confident. She adds that students feel more equal, and more respectful of each other. As for the possible violation of First Amendment rights, legal experts claim that the courts, which have become more conservative in recent years, may uphold "uniform" policies if they are considered necessary to maintain order in the schools and protect the health and safety of students.

• **Bring in guest speakers.** Elementary school is not too early to bring in gang specialists to talk to students about the dangers of gang life. Speakers can be police officers or even former gang members. Talks should be held in individual classrooms, not large auditoriums or gymnasiums. This will allow a more personal, one-on-one interaction with students. It's difficult to get the undivided attention of 800 fidgety students.

• **Offer gang seminars for parents,** educating them about gangs and suggesting ways they can combat gang activity. Get the parents on your side. Mail them flyers with information on gangs written in English, Spanish, and any other languages that are used in your community. (Sending this information home with the child has obvious drawbacks.)

• **Train all teachers and auxiliary personnel,** such as food service, maintenance, and library staff, to recognize gang signs and gang activity. Instruct them to report any such activity, as well as the youths involved, to security personnel and school administration officials.

• **Identify and pay attention to known gang leaders** and students who have transferred in from other schools because of gang-related activity. Maintain open lines of communication; talk to them on a regular basis. Try to keep them on the school's side. This is not to say that schools should bend rules or offer privileges to accommodate gang leaders. But it will be to a school's advantage to develop a rapport with these individuals, within established school policy. This is a good way to keep an eye on gang members, and they may be able to clue you in on gang events before they happen.

• **Beef up security with police patrols or additional security personnel,** particularly if your school has a substantial gang population. Some schools enforce what's called a closed campus. No one leaves or enters the school once classes have begun, unless they pass through security and have written authorization. A closed campus helps prevent students from going to their cars during lunch periods and between classes, which, along with after-school periods, are prime times for gang activity in schools. Gang members have used these times to recruit new members or settle a score from a wrong done during the first few class periods. Dropouts and expelled students who belong to a gang tend to visit schools during these periods to recruit, see boyfriends and girlfriends, and fight with rival gang members who are still in school. Extra security personnel or a closed campus policy will help eliminate these problems.

Have security staff station themselves at the doors to meet arriving guests and look for gang members who may try to visit fellow gang members during school hours. Once a school decides to hire security personnel, there are important skills and guidelines that these staff members should follow.

Security personnel should not:

• Reprimand a student or gang member in front of other students. The same goes for teachers. If you must reprimand, do so in private. A student who is disciplined or admonished in front of his or her peers may try to "save face" by talking back or becoming physically aggressive. This action can escalate to a dangerous level in a matter of seconds.

• Joke around with students. By engaging in horseplay or becoming one of them, a security staff member not only loses credibility, but may find him or herself pushed around emotionally. If a security staff member befriends a student, and then later finds him or herself in the awkward position of having to discipline that student, the student will play this friendship against the staff member. The security officer is no longer an authority figure.

• Call a gang member by his or her street moniker. Not only does this reinforce the gang member's status among peers, but the gang member may try to live up to his or her label. Security staff should also never allow students to address them by their first name. Again, this leads to a loss of credibility.

Security personnel should:

• Know the school's rules and policies regarding discipline. Security staff who don't know the rules as well at the students do will set themselves up for confrontations. When a student must be disciplined, be impartial and fair.

• Know the current fads that are popular in the community. This includes clothing, hair styles, and slang words. Security personnel should be able to distinguish normal sports apparel from that which has been altered by a gang member, They should be able to recognize gang hand signs, specific gang words, tattoos, and other identifiers found in this book (see Part Three).

• Look for gang members and other students who are under the influence of alcohol or drugs. Security staff should be knowledgeable about the types of drugs that are popular in the area, as well as the effects those drugs have on the body. Staff should look for students who exhibit hyperactivity, bloodshot eyes, slurred speech, incessant talking, disorientation, problems with coordination, and other symptoms of drug use.

• Watch and listen. Talk with the students when walking the halls. Listen for any rumors that might become problems later on. For example, rumors that outside gang members may be coming to the school or that two students may be meeting after school to fight are red flags that should be addressed by security staff immediately. Formulate a plan. If two students begin to square off, seek assistance from other school personnel, but do not dash to the scene. Students will be drawn to the confrontation if they see security staff running. Staff should learn to read students' faces. When students know a fight is forthcoming, they may congregate and talk excitedly to one another. Again, watch and listen. Anticipate fights before they begin.

• Maintain a good relationship with local law enforcement officials. By communicating frequently with the police, security staff can learn the latest gang fads or symbols, which gangs are currently at war, which members attend the school, and which new gangs are being formed. Strong relationships with law enforcement officials come in handy when police are needed to quell disturbances on campus; and schools can keep police up to date on any rumors about future gang activity that may take place off school grounds.

Gang Assessment Tool

Ronald D. Stevens from the National School Safety Center developed a questionnaire to help school and law enforcement officials determine if there is a gang presence in their community. The Gang Assessment Tool will assist schools and community officials in the evaluation process. Explanations or comments by Mr. Stevens are noted. Each of the following questions has a point value, and points are to be tallied up at the end of the questionnaire.

1. Do you have graffiti on or near your campus? (5 points)

Graffiti is one of the first warning signs of gang activity. If you have graffiti in your community or on your campus, you probably have gang activity.

2. Do you have crossed-out graffiti on or near your campus? (10 points)

At an elementary school in Los Angeles, five different graffiti monikers were present on the schoolhouse door. Each of the previous ones had been crossed out. The principal apologized for the graffiti, stating that (professional) painters had not been to the campus since the previous Friday; this was only Monday. Crossed-out graffiti indicates that more than one gang is in the community and the likelihood of gang warfare is higher.

3. Do your students wear colors, jewelry, or clothing; flash hand signals; or display other behavior that may be gang related? (10 points)

Dress styles, hand signs, jewelry, and other identifying marks reinforce members' affiliation with a particular gang. More and more school districts are establishing dress codes that prohibit the wearing of gang symbols, gang colors, or disruptive dress styles. Parents should be particularly aware of gang styles and colors and make certain their children do not wear them. It is all too easy to be mistaken for a gang member, and the consequences could be fatal.

4. Are drugs available at or near your school? (5 points)

Drugs and gangs are inseparably related. Some gangs are developing tremendous expertise in drug trafficking and sales. They have their own experts in money laundering, marketing, distribution, recruiting, and law. A gang will move into a community and provide the rent, utilities, telephone, and a starter kit of supplies to help members get the drug-trafficking operation going. Gangs are on the move and looking for new opportunities, perhaps in your community.

5. Has there been a significant increase in the number of physical confrontations/stare downs within the past 12 months in or near your school? (5 points)

Fights symbolize the increasing conflict on many campuses. School violence and intimidation encourage gang formation and gang-related activity. It is important to clearly communicate, consistently enforce, and fairly apply reasonable behavioral standards.

6. Are weapons increasingly present in your community? (10 points)

Weapons are the tools of the trade for gangs. Wherever gangs are found, weapons will follow. Unfortunately, when a weapon is used, an irreversible consequence and a chain reaction often result. A fistfight is one thing, but a gunfight can have a tragic outcome—and the violence usually only escalates.

7. Do your students use beepers, pagers, or cellular phones? (10 points)

The trend is for schools increasingly to outlaw the use of such devices by students. Most students are not doctors or lawyers and do not need beepers. Except in rare cases, beepers and pagers are inappropriate and unnecessary for students.

8. Has there been a drive-by shooting at or near your school? (15 points)

Drive-by shootings reflect more advanced gang-related problems. It is possible to have a gang presence in your community without drive-by shootings. Most of those shootings are the result of competition between rival gangs for drug turf or territorial control of a specific area. Once gang rivalry begins, it often escalates to increasing levels of violence. If you have had a drive-by shooting on or near your school campus, conditions are grave and gang activity in your community has escalated to its most serious state.

9. Have you had a "show-by" display of weapons at or near your school? (10 points)

Before you have a drive-by shooting, a "show-by"—a flashing of weapons—usually will occur. About the best course of action when such an incident happens is to duck and look for cover.

The head football coach in a suburban Portland, Oregon, community told of a recent incident in which a group of Crips, dressed in blue, came speeding through his school's field house parking lot. It was near the end of the day. His team was with him when he shouted, "Slow it down, fellas." They did, only to pull out a semi-automatic weapon and point it at the coach and his team. The coach had the good judgment to hit the deck and order his team to drop for cover. The coach said, "I thought I had bought the farm. Fortunately, they didn't pull the trigger. In my 20 years of teaching, I have never been afraid until this year."

A North Carolina teacher, a veteran of 18 years, related that her mother offered to buy out her teaching contract if only she would leave the profession. School violence has motivated some of the nation's best teachers to pull out.

10. Is your truancy rate increasing? (5 points)

There is a high correlation between truancy and daytime burglary. Excellent examples of truancy prevention and intervention programs are in effect in Houston, Texas; Rohnert Park, California; and Honolulu, Hawaii. Youngsters who are not in school often are terrorizing the community. Cooperation between schools and law enforcement to keep kids in school is important.

11. Are an increasing number of racial incidents occurring in your community or school? (5 points)

A high correlation exists between gang membership and racial conflict. We have often treated new immigrants and people from diverse cultural and ethnic backgrounds poorly and thus have encouraged the formation of gangs. Many gangs are formed along racial and ethnic lines for purposes of protection and affiliation. Sometimes friendship and affiliation take a backseat to criminal acts of violence and intimidation. People want to be respected and appreciated. It is important to cultivate multicultural understanding and respect that embraces diversity.

12. Does your community have a history of gangs? (10 points)

Gangs are not a new phenomenon. They have been around for decades, in some cases, for generations. Youth gangs are even mentioned in the Bible (2 Kings 2:23). If your community has a history of gangs, your children are much more likely to be influenced by them.

13. Is there an increasing presence of informal social groups with unusual names like "the Woodland Heights Posse," "Rip Off a Rule," "Kappa Phi Nasty," "18th Street Crew," or "Females Simply Chillin"? (15 points)

The development of hard-core gang members often begins in groups with innocent and yet revealing names. Youngsters in these groups often become primary recruiting targets for hard-core gang members.

Scoring

A score of 15 points or less indicates that the school or community does not have a significant gang problem and there is no need for alarm. A score of 20 to 40 points indicates an emerging gang problem. Gang factors and related incidents should be closely monitored, and a gang plan should be developed. A score of 45 to 60 points indicates the need to immediately establish a comprehensive, systematic gang prevention and intervention plan. A score of 65 points or more indicates an acute gang problem that merits a total gang prevention, intervention, and suppression program.

Chapter 13

INDIVIDUAL RESPONSE

> Now hold onto yourselves. There is one more thing. A terrible presence is in there with her, so much rage, so much betrayal. I've never sensed anything like it. I don't know what's come over this house, but it was strong enough to punch a hole into this world and take your daughter away from you. It lies to her. It says things only a child could understand. It's been using her to restrain the others. To her, it simply is another child. To us, it is the Beast. . . . Now let's go get your daughter.
>
> From the movie *Poltergeist*

Schools and law enforcement officials can't fight the problem of gangs alone. The strongest way to combat the gang problem is to meet it face-to-face on the home front. The first thing we as parents must do is take a deep breath and admit that gangs are here to stay and that children, including ours, will be exposed to them. Period. There is no getting around it. From the music they hear to the movies and television they watch, kids are exposed to the notion that violence is an acceptable way to settle differences.

Hollywood has a long history of glamorizing gangsters and gangster violence. Producers know that many teenagers enjoy action and violence in movies. They also know that teenagers make up the largest segment of the movie-going public, and they will continue to make movies that capture the teen market.

Gang members and troubled teenagers seem to be a popular subject matter on daytime talk shows, as well. Sitting on stage, detached and defiant, civility and manners give way to cockiness and rudeness. What's sad is that the teenager on stage is usually pitted against his or her parent or some other adult figure, and heated exchanges take place. The shows' producers love it, the audience loves it, and despite what journalists write about these shows and the people who watch them, the viewers love it. Unfortunately, these daytime talk shows tend to air when many children are returning home from school, possibly to an empty house.

Once we accept the unfortunate reality that gangs are here to stay, we can start to do something. Remember, we are the adults here. Now is the time to reclaim our children. It is our responsibility to train them, set an example, and provide the guidance they need to avoid gangs and gang activity.

No matter how scary it may be, we must face the reality of gangs. To deny it would be of absolutely no value to our children. The following are ideas about how we can take back our children. You may disagree with me on some. That's okay. If one suggestion doesn't work or is not to your liking, try another. The worst thing a parent can do is to do nothing. Like schools, parents must take a proactive approach. It won't be easy. Raising children and directing them away from life's dangers is complex, time consuming, and sometimes intimidating. Confrontations can be painful, but in this case, they could save lives.

1. Clothes: Pay attention to the clothes your child wears. Does he or she have a great deal of clothes of the same color, or of certain color combinations (such as black and blue or black and gold)? This may indicate gang interest or involvement. (For more information on clothing and gang colors, see Chapters 7 and 8.)

2. Jewelry: Is your child wearing a lot of gold jewelry? Is his or her jewelry the type worn by gangs? How was it purchased? Where did the money come from? (For information on gang jewelry, see Chapter 8.)

3. Wallets and purses: Some of the larger gangs issue business cards. Check your child's wallet or purse if you suspect gang involvement. Also, be suspicious if your child has large amounts of unexplained cash. If the child claims that he or she has a job, ask to see a paycheck stub.

4. Gang symbols: Parents should look for gang symbols, names, or graffiti on schoolbooks, notebooks, clothes, and tattoos. If your child hesitates when confronted, or says that he or she is in a club, be suspicious. (Refer to Chapter 8 for specific symbols and other identifiers.)

5. Pocket pagers and portable phones: If your child carries a pocket pager or portable phone, does he or she really need it? Gang members use pagers for a host of reasons, including to contact one another and set up drug deals. In a Chicago suburb in 1995, a student who was in a gang was ambushed and killed while sitting in the back of a driver's education car, waiting to take a road test. A rival gang member was also in the car, taking his road test. The driver's education teacher was unaware of this dangerous combination. The gang member asked the teacher if he could stop to make an emergency phone call to his mother. The teacher unwittingly allowed the request, and the caller paged another gang member to carry out the ambush and killing.

Some schools have banned pocket pagers and portable phones for that very reason. And guess what? The students haven't fallen over dead without them. You can ban them, too. If you have to contact your child after school, schedule a time that your child can call you at work or at home. You can even arrange a daily "check-in" call.

6. Role model: Try to be a positive role model. Are you in a gang? If so, why? Do you want your child to follow your path?

How's your drug and alcohol consumption? If you instruct your children on the dangers of gangs or drug and alcohol abuse, but are involved with them yourself, it's time to step back and take a look at yourself. You must set the example.

7. Free time: Many teenagers have excessive amounts of unstructured, unsupervised time on their hands. Whenever you can, participate in positive activities with your child. If you are a single parent, you may want to have friends or other family members spend quality time with your child. Help from family and friends, however, can never replace the time you spend with your son or daughter.

8. Neighborhood watch: Parents can be involved with neighborhood watch organizations and gang graffiti removal projects. Ask local city officials and law enforcement personnel about how to organize a neighborhood gang watch, or find out if such programs are already available. Organizations such as MAG (Mothers Against Gangs) may have local chapters.

9. Church: Your local church may offer programs or assistance for dealing with gangs. Many churches, particularly in the inner city, have after-school activities and projects geared toward at-risk youths.

10. Bedroom: Search your child's bedroom. You have the right. It's your house. One woman suspected her son might be involved with a gang, but she wasn't sure. Even though she felt like she was trespassing, she searched his bedroom. There she found a new twenty-five inch color TV, a VCR, and money—lots of money. Mostly in small denominations, the money was stuffed in a sock drawer and hidden between his mattress and box springs. The woman was astounded, but thankful that she had put aside her reluctance to violate her son's privacy. He did not have a job, and he had a lot of explaining to do. In this case, the woman made good use of her extended family—she called upon a number of her son's uncles and cousins for help. This showed the young man that there were family members who cared, and the woman didn't have to face the problem alone.

Certainly, snooping is not recommended unless you suspect gang involvement, drug use, or other serious activities. But if you are suspicious, this is not the time to tiptoe around and be timid. Snoop, and confront.

11. Ask questions: Ask lots of questions. This is especially true when it comes to your child's friends or free time. Some specific questions are:

- *Where are you going?* Ask for specifics. "Just out" is not an acceptable answer.
- *When will you be home?* Set a curfew and enforce it. Do not allow your children to stay out late, on the streets.
- *Who are your friends?* Know who your child is spending time with. Notice what they are wearing. Be suspicious if your child doesn't want you to meet his or her friends, or refuses to talk about what they do together.
- *What's your favorite music group?* Acquaint yourself with the latest "gangsta" rap music favored by gangs. Not all rap music is gang-oriented, but it's a good idea to be informed. Pick up a CD case and read the lyrics. Also, look for the Parent Advisory label. This means the lyrics contain strong and/or sexually explicit language. If the lyrics match your child's slang or attitude, you may have cause for concern. The same can be said for music favored by Skinheads. (Refer to Chapter 7 for information on Skinhead music.)
- *What do you know about gangs?* You may be surprised at your child's answer. If children attend a school with a strong gang presence, they may know quite a bit. If your child is evasive, it may mean that he or she has more than a passing interest in gangs. Some kids will come right out and admit to being in a gang.
- *Do you know how much you're needed in this family?* Children need to know they are important. Tell them you love them! If you

don't accept your child or make him or her feel important and wanted, the gangs are more than happy to do it for you. It's your choice.

12. School: Monitor children's grades closely. If your child's grades are slipping but his or her attendance is good, provide a well-lit, quiet place in your home for studying. If your child is habitually truant, he or she may be skipping school to hang out with friends. This means that your child is vulnerable to gang recruitment—if he or she isn't involved with a gang already. Participate in your child's schooling. Monitor and offer assistance with homework. Check with the attendance office periodically. Your involvement tells your child you care.

13. Funerals: I hope and pray that no parents reading this book will ever have to bury a son or daughter because of gang activity. In the event that you do, however, do not allow fellow gang members to attend the funeral. All too often, the news media record scenes of a gang member being laid to rest while fellow gang members file by, dressed in gang colors, flashing gang signs to their slain comrade for the last time. In my opinion, to allow gang members to pay their respects labels and cheapens the life of the deceased. To die for a gang is a noble cause? Where is the honor in that? Funerals should be for family and relatives.

14. Police: Parents of gang members may be all too familiar with local police stations. Some gang members as young as twelve or thirteen have multiple arrests or are already on probation. Remember, if your child has chosen to become involved with gangs, it is his or her decision. Now, having said that, there are a number of ways parents can respond to a child who has been arrested. The following two methods are sure to send a message:

Some parents refuse to pick their children up from the police station. If your child is involved with gangs and is of legal age (the age at which you are no longer legally responsible for him or her), consider letting your child sit in jail. Visit, or write your child a letter, but let the gang bail him or her out. It may sound callous, but it lets your child know you will not tolerate involvement with gangs. If the gang does not provide bail, chances are they won't visit either. When gang members find themselves abandoned by their gang "family," they are more likely to leave it.

If your child is a minor, a loud word of CAUTION is in order. Child welfare agencies take a dim view of parents who refuse to take custody of their children. In fact, parents may face charges of neglect—and could lose parental rights—if they refuse to pick their child up from a police station. Some parents are simply at their breaking point, especially if the child has had numerous arrests. This is understandable. But remember, if your child is a minor, you have a legal obligation to pick him or her up from the police station, or face painful, often irreparable consequences later.

Some parents will pick their children up, but will let them sit in jail awhile and sweat it out first. Rather than jump into your car and rush to your child's rescue, consider taking your time, deliberately slowing the process. It forces the child to sit and wait and wonder. Granted, this approach often frustrates police, who have to wait for the parents. But the child will feel the impact. This method is most effective for children who are young and just experimenting with gangs, but are not yet fully entrenched. It may not always work in a family whose child is older, has had a number of arrests, and is more familiar with law enforcement procedures.

15. Drugs: Educate yourself about illicit drugs—their street names, how people use them, their effects, and the tools people use to take them. There are volumes of drug literature readily available from schools, youth centers, police departments, and other community organizations. Try to find books with illustrations so you will know what to look for.

Some gangs sell drugs exclusively; it is the reason for their existence. However, most street gangs sell drugs as only a small, although important, part of their everyday activities. Gangs sell drugs to raise money for weapons, bail, parties, and other expenses, and bloody turf wars are fought between gangs trying to get a foothold on new drug distribution areas.

16. Listen: Perhaps the most important thing you can do for your child is to listen. Really listen. Listen to what your child says, and listen to what goes unsaid. Listen for slang words associated with gangs, and ask the child what the words mean. Tell your child that you are concerned. Tell your child that you suspect he or she may be involved in gang activity, because you have noticed some of the identifiers explained in this book. Your child might actually be relieved. He or she may privately want to leave the gang but not know how. If your child is in a gang, ask if he or she has thought about leaving it. Keep the lines of communication open. Lend an ear, then take control. It can be done. And your child is going to need you every step of the way.

Appendix One

VICE LORD MANIFESTO

Many of the highly-structured gangs have gang manifestos, establishing rules, symbols, the chain of command, and so forth. The following Vice Lord manifesto, which police confiscated from gang members, is an excellent example of the level of organization achieved by many gangs.

ALMIGHTY VICE LORD NATION
CHAIN OF COMMAND

THE FOLLOWING IS THE ADMINISTRATIVE ORGANIZATION OF THE ALMIGHTY VICE LORD NATION . . . IT IS THE CHAIN OF COMMAND AND SHALL BE FOLLOWED AT ALL TIMES!!

Chief Elite
The Chief Elite has superiority over the entire body of the Organization. He brings in the overall decision. He is the Supreme Authority of the ALMIGHTY VICE LORD NATION. The duty of the Chief Elite is to formulate the Laws and Rules of the ALMIGHTY VICE LORD NATION that keep the Organization moving in an organized and constructive manner at all times no matter what the circumstance of environment may be!

Minister of Justice
The Chief Minister exercises his function in a Judgment-like fashion. He determines right—Justice—from wrong—Injustice—on a balance scale. He shall speak on behalf of the Chief Elite. He shall make sure that everyone in the ALMIGHTY VICE LORD NATION is being treated right at all times. He is the only one in Authority to take orders from the Chief Elite. He shall make sure they are carried out efficiently and accurately. He and the Elites are the only ones authorized to approach the Chief Elite about any problems pertaining to the ALMIGHTY VICE LORD NATION.

Elites
The Elite shall be assigned to a particular location in which they are in charge and shall exercise their authority as such. For example, if an Elite is in charge of the ALMIGHTY VICE LORD NATION Finance, his only priority is to deal with the Finance Department and carry himself in the highest manner of a Vice Lord and to give constructive and positive advice only when needed or asked from other location Elites. He will be always honored and respected as an Elite. If a problem arises which calls for an immediate decision, and no one can reach the Minister of Justice nor the Chief Elite, then the problem shall be taken to the nearest Elite.

Minister of Command
These chosen men are the Elites also, however, we come to certain situations where Representatives can and will fulfill this position if he is qualified and voted into the position by the location Elite—however, he is commanded to make sure that the Laws and Rules are functioning properly in the order

EIGHT PRINCIPLES OF LAW

I, as a representative of the ALMIGHTY VICE LORD NATION swear with my life never to dishonor our most High Chief, Minister of Justice, Elites, or any other representative of the ALMIGHTY VICE LORD NATION.

I, as a representative of the ALMIGHTY VICE LORD NATION, will teach our people, protect our people, love our people, and if it is the will of our ALMIGHTY GOD ALLAH, Die for our people, so that one day they will walk with the "Golden" path of Vice Lords as free people, as productive people, as people progressing in the love of Vice Lords, the knowledge of Vice Lords, the wisdom of Vice Lords, the understanding of Vice Lords, the living of Vice Lords.

I, as a representative of the ALMIGHTY VICE LORD NATION will never stray from the truthful teachings of our most wise and beloved Elites.

I, as a representative of the ALMIGHTY VICE LORD NATION, will help my people with any problem they may encounter be it mental or physical, for their problems are my problems, and my problems are theirs.

I, as a representative of the ALMIGHTY VICE LORD NATION, will never take the word of another before that of any representative of the ALMIGHTY VICE LORD NATION. This I swear upon the Vice Lord Nation.

I, as a representative of the ALMIGHTY VICE LORD NATION, swear with my life that I will never put anything or anyone before my High Chief, Minister of Justice, Elites, or any representative of the ALMIGHTY VICE LORD NATION, be it my life my family, or associates.

I, as a representative of the ALMIGHTY VICE LORD NATION, will never deny any Vice Lord materially or spiritually, under any circumstances at all, or be denied.

I, as a representative of the ALMIGHTY VICE LORD NATION, swear with my life that I will not lie on any representative of the ALMIGHTY VICE LORD NATION, fight any representative, steal from any representative, or take by force anything from any representative of the ALMIGHTY VICE LORD NATION.

BEHOLD
ALMIGHTY VICE LORD NATION

VICE LORD NATION CODE OF CONDUCT

Respect
Every Elite, Minister, and Representative of the ALMIGHTY VICE LORD NATION will at all times give proper respect to every other Representative of our Organization. We will respect every representative of every other organization, and every Vice Lord will demand, by his conduct, character, personal demeanor and action and deeds, respect in return. Every Elite, Minister, and Representative of the ALMIGHTY VICE LORD NATION will always give respect to persons who are not representatives of any Nation. Disrespect is a very serious violation of the Principles of Law of the ALMIGHTY VICE LORD NATION and will be judged accordingly, therefore, it will not be tolerated.

Discipline
Discipline must, and will be maintained for the successful functioning of the Nation. Every order you are given is to be carried out promptly and efficiently. Every order you receive has a specific reason and will not be questioned unless a Representative doesn't understand the specific order being given—this is the only justification in questioning an order! Failure to carry out an order promptly and efficiently could endanger the life of yourself or other Vice Lords. For this reason, orders will be obeyed accurately! Failure to do so will result in Disciplinary action appropriate for the situation being taken immediately.

Meetings
General meetings of the ALMIGHTY VICE LORD NATION are held for the purpose of Nation Business, and will be conducted accordingly. During all meetings the Elite will be the first to state the business of the Nation. They will be followed by the members of the administration of the Nation. After they have stated their Nation Business, each Representative of the ALMIGHTY VICE LORD NATION will be given the opportunity to speak

about matters germane to those being discusses at the meeting. When any Vice Lord is speaking during meetings, every other Vice Lord will remain quiet and attentive, failure to do so constitutes disrespect and will result in immediate disciplinary action. All problems pertaining to any location shall be discussed when all important factors are discussed first. All Elites, Ministers, Representatives will remain on their square while meetings are in progress. Smoking will be refrained from ALL meetings! All Elites and Ministers will attend location meetings unless their occupation makes it impossible!

Dues

The ALMIGHTY VICE LORD NATION Boxes are established for the benefit of every Vice Lord. We all have times of need for ourselves and family, and having these boxes help meet these needs. Therefore, dues will be paid by every Vice Lord no less than monthly. The ALMIGHTY VICE LORD NATION dues will be paid on the 15th of each and every month unless an exception has been made by the location Elite. Failure for any Elite, Minister, or Representative to pay dues will result in a loss of box privileges, and possible disciplinary actions. If any Representative can't pay his monthly dues, he will offer himself to the service of the Nation in some constructive manner—ONLY if it is impossible for him to pay his dues. Anything taken from the Box for personal use must be replaced no later than the 15th of the following month. If Representatives have an accurate account on paying their dues, they have all the right to borrow a sufficient amount from the box for constructive use—These boxes are for the use and benefit of every Vice Lord—treat them as such!

Horseplay

Horseplay is one of the principle causes leading to disrespect and can therfor result in other serious problems. To avoid such problems, horseplay will be kept to a bare minimum—the yard and the gym is the place to play, The manner in which one Vice Lord conducts himself for others to see reflects not only upon his character, but the character of THE ENTIRE ALMIGHTY VICE LORD NATION.

Fighting

While it is the unspoken obligation of every Vice Lord to defend himself or every other Vice Lord, to the extent of giving his life if necessary, no member of the ALMIGHTY VICE LORD NATION will place himself in any situation where he is needlessly involved in fights over trivial matters. If any Vice Lord is attacked it is the sworn duty of every other Vice Lord to overcome his attacker by any means necessary. If any Elite, Minister, or Representative takes it in their own hands to fight among themselves it will be a violation of all our Laws of the ALMIGHTY VICE LORD NATION and will be dealt with immediately. Therefore, no Representative of the ALMIGHTY VICE LORD NATION is ever to fight among themselves unless it is authorized with boxing gloves in the circle.

Movement
If anytime you make a housing, cell, location, or work transfer, you will notify the location Elite of that transfer at the earliest possible time. To maintain security and ensure ready access to All Vice Lords, it is mandatory that we are always aware of the work and location assignments of every member of the ALMIGHTY VICE LORD NATION. Upon moving anywhere in institution, each specific location will move as one in a way.

SUMMARY

This CODE OF CONDUCT is established for the purpose of maintaining security, discipline, safety, and integrity of the ALMIGHTY VICE LORD NATION, you are expected to know and observe this code at all times. AT ALL TIMES, BE AWARE OF YOUR SURROUNDING AND THE PEOPLE AROUND YOU!! AT ALL TIMES REMEMBER WHO YOU ARE, WHAT YOU ARE, AND CONDUCT YOURSELF ACCORDINGLY.

ALMIGHTY VICE LORD NATION

Appendix Two

SLANG GLOSSARY AND NUMBER CODES

Gang members use slang to prevent others, particularly law enforcement personnel, from understanding their communication. Please note that this list is not complete. Slang changes as some words are phased out and new ones are introduced. Also, be aware that a lot of slang language is not necessarily gang related, but is used frequently by young people in the course of everyday conversation. The following terms are used across the United States.

Slang Glossary

AA: Aid and assist

Above board: Honest and truthful

Ace: A backup person or best friend

All is one: Motto of unity used by members of the Folk Nation

All is well: Motto of unity used by members of the People Nation

A fair one: Fighting between gangs according to set rules (used infrequently)

Baile: To fight (used by Hispanic gangs)

Baller: A big drug dealer (used by Bloods)

Bangin': Gang banging, being in a gang

Barrio: Neighborhood (used by Hispanic gangs)

Base head: Person hooked on cocaine

Beemer: A BMW automobile

Belittle yourself: To misrepresent gang affiliation by giving false hand signs (same as false flagging)

Benzo: A Mercedes Benz automobile

BG: Baby gangster

Big boy: A higher-up gang member

Big time: A large number of gang members

BIH: Burn in hell

Bit: Time in jail

BKA: Blood Killers Always (used by Crips in their graffiti)

Blade: Knife

Blanca: Females (used by Hispanic gangs)

Blob: A derogatory name for Bloods (used by Crips)

Blood: A fellow gang member, faction, family

Blowman: A gang member chosen to shoot a gun

Boned out: To leave or quit

Book: To run away, leave

Booyah: The sound of a shotgun

Braces: Suspenders (used by Skinheads)

Brand: Tattoo

Breakdown: Shotgun

Bucket: An older, beat-up automobile

Bud: Marijuana

Bullet: One year in jail or prison

Bumper kit: A female's butt

Bumpin': Describes something that looks good; describes a car stereo that has large woofers which, when played loud enough, allow the bass to reverberate and shake the car

Bumping titties: Fighting

Burn: To steal or cheat

Burner: A gang member known for shooting

Bussin': To shoot at an opposing gang member

Bust a cap: To shoot at an opposing gang member

Buster: A wanna-be gang member

Busting: Using fists or weapons in a fight

Buzzed: Being high or drunk

Caca: Drugs

Calling the shots: To act as an authority figure in a gang

Calo: Slang that is in both Spanish and English combined (used by Hispanic gangs)

Camarada: Bro; *see* Homeboy (used by Hispanic gangs)

Canton: Residence, crib

Can you dig it?: Can you understand?

Cap: Shoot (to shoot someone is to cap someone)

Carcel: Penitentiary (used by Hispanic gangs)

Carnal: Brother in unity (used by Hispanic gangs)

Carrucha: An automobile (used by Hispanic gangs)

Catch a cold: To get killed

Chante: Residence (used by Hispanic gangs)

Chavala: Girlfriend (used by Hispanic gangs)

Check it out: Listen to what I have to say

Chillin': Kicking back, relaxing

Chill out: Stop, don't do that

Chipping: Occasional use of narcotics

Cholo: Crazy life; male gang member (used by Hispanic gangs)

Chota: Police (used by Hispanic gangs)

Chuco: Veteran gang member (used by Hispanic gangs)

CK: Crip Killer (used by Bloods in their graffiti)

Claim: To announce your gang affiliation

Claim jumpers: People who falsely claim gang membership

Clica: Gang, set (used by Hispanic gangs)

Cluckhead: A crack addict

Colors: Gang colors, usually found on clothing

Compa: Friend (from *compadre*, used by Hispanic gangs)

Condado: Local jail (used by Hispanic gangs)

Controlla: We control (used by Hispanic gangs)

Constitution: Written rules, history of the gang

Co-Sign: To approve

Courting in: Initiating someone into a gang

Courting out: Expelling someone from a gang

Crank: Speed (drug); a mentally unstable person

Crab: A derogatory name for Crips (used by Bloods)

Crib: House, jail cell, apartment

Crippin': Gang banging (used by Crips)

Crossover: To go over to another gang

Cruzales: A derogatory name for Folks (used by the People Nation)

Cuate: Friend (used by Hispanic gangs)

Curb serving: Selling crack cocaine on a street corner

Custer: A false gang member

Cuzz: A name Crips call one another (from the word *cousin*)

Dai lo: Leader of a Chinese gang

Dancing: Fighting

Dead President: Money

Dead rag: A red handkerchief (used by Bloods)

Deep: Heavy conversation; large membership

Demonstration: A fight between gangs

Deuce and a quarter (or half): A Buick 225

Deuce-deuce (or double deuce): A .22 caliber gun

Die for the turf: To defend one's gang territory, show loyalty

Dis, Dissin': To put down or act disrespectfully toward someone

Do a ghost: To leave the scene

Dogging: Treating someone poorly

Donde?: Where are you from? (used by Hispanic gangs)

Donut: A derogatory name for Disciples (used by Vice Lords)

Dope: Excellent, sounds great

Do-rag (du-rag): A handkerchief, usually of gang colors, often worn on the head

Down (for the set): Loyal to the group, ready to fight or shoot

Down for mine: Having the ability to protect oneself

Drag: Having the ability to sweet talk females

Draped: Wearing a lot of gold jewelry

Drop a dime: To snitch or tell on someone, call the cops

Dropping the flag: Leaving the gang

Drywall: A false or impure drug that looks like crack cocaine: crushed Alka Seltzer and aspirin, for example

Dusted: Beat someone in a race, killed someone

Encerrado: Locked up (used by Hispanic gangs)

Enforcer: A gang member who dispenses discipline

E-Rickette: A derogatory name for Crips (used by Bloods)

Ese: Exclamation for "Hey Man!" (used by Hispanic gangs)

Essay: A Hispanic gang member

Everything is everything: All is okay

Expecting rain and thunder: Looking for trouble

Faded: Showing disrespect

False flagging: Showing false gang affiliation, usually through hand signs

Federated: A term used by Crips to show disrespect for the color red (the Bloods' color)

Fell down: Stabbed

Five High–Six Die: A Vice Lord term to show contempt for the Disciples (represents five-point star vs. six-point star)

Fire up: To shoot at someone

Firing on someone: Shooting at someone or throwing a punch

Five-O: Cops (from the TV show *Hawaii Five-O*)

Flakes: A derogatory name for Latin Kings (used by Folks)

Flashing: Displaying gang hand signs

Flowers: Female Cobra Stones

Flue rag: A blue handkerchief

Fly: Good looking

Flying your colors: Representing your gang colors

Folks Poppin'–People Droppin': A term used to insult the People Nation (used by Folks)

Four-five: A .45 caliber gun

Freak: A good-looking female

Fresh: Good looking

Frog: A female of low morals (jumps into any male's car)

From the shoulder: To fight

Front, front off: To show off by putting someone down

Furniture: Knives

Futures: Young gang members

Game: Criminal activity

Gang banger: A member of a gang

Gang banging: Being involved in gang activity

Gat: Gun

Gauge: Shotgun

G-dare: Daring someone to do something

Geek: Someone who is high

Gee'd up: Dressed up gangster style, showing gang colors

Get down: To fight

Get jammed: To be confronted

Get off my case: Leave me alone

Get out of my face: Leave me alone, get away (more serious)

Getting busy: To do any activity that is considered dangerous (robbery, drive-by shootings, and so forth)

Getting into the groove: Getting things done

Ghetto Star: Gang leader

Gig: A job (from stage performers' usage); a gathering

Girl: Homosexual

Going to visit Lugo: Going to be killed

Good Monks: Good people

Go off: To act crazy

Ghosting: Leaving the area

G-name: A gangster's street name

Grease: To kill someone

G-ride (Gangster ride): A stolen car

Grip: Having or trying to obtain money

Growing daisies: Dead

Got it going on: To be a successful person

G-ster: Shortened term for gangster

Gump: Homosexual

Gunned up: Having an arsenal of guns

Hangin', Bangin', and Slangin': Hanging out, gang banging, and selling dope

Hard look: A hard stare

Hat up: To leave the scene

Headup: To start a fight

He's from nowhere: He's not a gang member

High beams on: To be high on cocaine

High five: A physical motion where one shows one's hands with all five fingers pointing upward (represents People Nation)

High Five–Six Die: A derogatory term insulting the Folks (used by the People)

High roller: A big drug dealer (used by Crips)

Holding it down: Defending one's turf, neighborhood, area

Ho: Whore

Homeboy, homey: Male associate gang member, friend, comrade

Homegirl: Female associate gang member, friend

Homes: *see* Homeboy

Homey: Someone from the neighborhood

Hood: Neighborhood

Hook: A derogatory name for Vice Lords (used by Folks)

Hooked up: Belonging to a certain gang

Hoo-rah: Talking loud

Hoopty: An automobile

Hubba: Crack cocaine

Hubba pigeon: Someone who picks up bits of crack cocaine that have fallen on the ground

Hustler: A person who is only out to make money and is not into gangs

Illing: Not thinking clearly, making mistakes

Inca: A gang president (used by Hispanic gangs)

Ink: A tattoo

In the mix: Involved with gang activity

Jack: To commit a holdup

Jackin': Using force to steal something

Jacked up: Confronted by someone, beat up, assaulted

Jammed up: In trouble

Jiving: Trying to fool someone

Jonesin': Going through drug withdrawal

Juice: Influence, power

Jumped in: Initiated into a gang (usually by being beaten by other gang members, killing a rival gang member, or participating in a drive-by shooting)

Jumped out: To have officially left a gang (usually after being beaten by fellow gang members)

Junior: A young gang member

Jura: Police (used by Hispanic gangs)

Kibbles and Bits: Small crumbs of cocaine

Kick you down: To set you up (get you in trouble) in the middle of a drug transaction

Kicking back: Relaxing, goofing off, killing time

Kicking your hat: Tilting one's hat a certain way

Killer: An extreme expression

Know where I'm coming from: Understand what I'm saying

Kool: It's okay

Lady: Girlfriend

La Raza: Hispanic race

Libre: Free (used by Hispanic gangs)

Let's bail: Let's get out of here

Lit up: To get shot or punched

Loc: Loco, crazy (used by Hispanic gangs)

Lok: *see* Loc (used by Bloods)

Love: Crack cocaine

Mad-dogging: Staring at someone in an antagonistic manner

Main man: Best friend, backup

Making bank: Making money (usually illegally)

The man: A law enforcement official

Manifesto: Written rules and history of the gang

Manotas: Police (used by Hispanic gangs)

Mata: Drugs (used by Hispanic gangs)

Mark: A wanna-be gang member

Married: Joined a gang

Midget: A young gang member

Mission: A drive-by shooting

Mobbing: Hanging out

Moniker: A gang member's street name

Moreno: Black (used by Hispanic gangs)

Mouth: Anyone who relays secret information

Mud duck: An ugly female

Mud People: A derogatory name for African Americans (used by Skinheads)

My shit: Drugs and drug paraphernalia, guns

Nada: Nothing (used by Hispanic gangs)

Nation: The gang as a whole

Neutron: A person who is not a gang member

Norte (or Norteño): North, usually used to describe northern California; someone who is from northern California (used by Hispanic gangs)

Not too much like 007: Playing it cool

Nut up: To be mad at someone

Off brands: Rival gangs

OG: Original Gangster, one who has earned his or her gang stripes

Oi: Skinhead greeting; type of Skinhead music

On line: Showing proper behavior

On the pipe: Freebasing crack cocaine

On the square (or strength): These are the facts

On the surface of things: On top of what's going on

On the up and up: These are the facts

One time: Police

Open the line: To begin communicating

Other side of the line: To join another gang

Outs: Out of prison (or any other detention facility)

Packing: Carrying a gun

Pay back: To get even

Pay the bills: To stab a person

Peanut butter: A derogatory name for Bloods (used by Crips)

Pee wee: A young gang member

People: Vice Lords and affiliates

Phildoras: Not expensive (used by Hispanic gangs)

Pica: Cocaine (used by Hispanic gangs)

Pimped out: Well dressed

Pinta: Prison (used by Hispanic gangs)

Pintada: Gang graffiti (used by Hispanic gangs)

Piru: Another name for a Blood

Placas: A gang member's street name, graffiti (used by Hispanic gangs)

Player: A ladies' man

Poo butt: A timid person, sissy

Polvo: Cocaine, usually in powder form (used by Hispanic gangs)

Poor box: A box or container of items collected by gang members as dues or payments for protection. The items are then distributed among members of the gang

Popped a cap (or can): *see* Bust a cap

Por vida: For life (used by Hispanic gangs)

Posse: Gang (used by East Coast gangs)

Primo: Great drugs

Proper: Sounds right

Puffer: A person who smokes cocaine

Pugging: Fighting

Pulling you on: Making a fool of you

Punk: Homosexual

Put 'em in check: To discipline someone

Put in work: *see* Getting busy

Putting you on: Making a fool of you

Put on front street: To snitch on someone

Puto: Homosexual (used by Hispanic gangs)

Puto mark: Crossing out or writing over another gang's graffiti (used by Hispanic gangs)

Rag: A handkerchief with gang colors

Raise: To leave

Ran up on: Robbed in a sneak attack

Rap: A style of music, to talk

Rap sheet: Record of criminal offenses

Rata: A snitch (used by Hispanic gangs)

Rat Packin': Ganging up on someone

Ray: A handkerchief with gang colors

Recruiting: Looking for good-looking girls

Red eye: A hard stare

Relative: *see* Homeboy (used by Bloods)

Rep: Reputation

Represent: To show gang affiliation

Ride: An automobile

Ride on: To go to a rival gang neighborhood, usually to fight or initiate a drive-by shooting

Rifa: Rules, written in graffiti, meaning "we control" or "we are the best" (used by Hispanic gangs)

Rifamos: This gang rules (used by Hispanic gangs)

Righteous: Upstanding, proper behavior

R.I.H.: Rest in Hell (used in graffiti as a threat to rival gang members)

R.I.P.: Rest in Peace (used in graffiti in remembrance of a fallen gang member or to challenge a rival gang member)

Rippin' and runnin': Committing crimes while living on the streets

Road dog: Best friend

Rock: Crack cocaine

Rocks, Rock Boy(s): A derogatory name for Cobra Stones and El Rukns (used by Folks)

Rod: A gun

Roll: A cigarette; to rob someone

Roll 'em up: To arrest, force out of the scene

Rollin': Making money

Roscoe: A gun (uncommon)

Ru (rooster): Piru

Sagging: The style of wearing pants low around the waist

Scag: An unattractive female; heroin

Scandalous: A lazy or bad person

Schooling: Education

School them: To instruct younger gang members

Scratch: Money

Section: An area where gang membership is large

Set: Any particular gang group, especially in a specific area or turf (used by Crips and Bloods)

Shank or shiv: Knife (mostly prison use)

Sherman stick: Marijuana cigarette laced with PCP

Shooter: A gang member who uses firearms

Shotcaller: Person in charge

Shot out: Recognized by a rival gang member

Signify: To put down, insult

Six Alive–Five Die: A term used to insult the People Nation (used by Folks)

Six Pop–Five Drop: A term used to insult the People Nation (used by Disciples)

Skeezer: An ugly female

Slanging: Selling drugs

Slippin': Not watching what's going on, being sloppy or careless

Slipping in the dark: Getting stabbed

Slob: A derogatory name for Bloods (used by Crips)

Slow your roll: Take it easy, kick back

Smoke 'em: Kill them

Smokes: Cigarettes

Snaps: Money

Snitch: An informant

Snoop: *see* Slob

Snow queen (bunny): A white female

Springs: An automobile

Squab: To argue

Square: A cigarette

Stack: Save it, put it away (usually money)

Stacking: Throwing another gang's sign upside down to show disrespect

Stall it out: Stop what you're doing

Stone: Expressing something to the fullest extent

Straight: Things are alright or understood fully

Straight up: Correct or honest

Strong: Large gang membership

'Sup?: What's up?

Sur (or Sureños): South, usually used to describe southern California (used by Hispanic gangs)

Tag: A graffiti signature

Tagbanger: A gang member who accompanies a Tagger, carries weapons, and fights members of other Tagger gangs

Tagging: Applying graffiti; wearing a cap with the price tag exposed

Take him out of the box: Kill him

Talking head: Wanting to fight, arguing

Talking smack: Talking in an aggressive manner

Tall: Large in numbers

TG (Tiny Gangster): Any very young gang member

Throw a switch: To misrepresent gang affiliation, usually through hand signs

Throw down the crown: A term used to insult Latin Kings (used by Folks)

Tight: Close to someone

Tip: Gang

Tonto: A stupid person

To the curb: In a bad position, getting rid of something

Torcido: Messing up (used by Hispanic gangs)

TOS: Terminate On Sight, a written order for the execution of a fellow or rival gang member

Toss up: A female used for sex

Trece: Thirteen; *see* Sur (used by Hispanic gangs)

Tres eight, three eight: A .38 caliber gun

Trick on someone: To inform on someone

Trip, tripping: Unbelievable, too much; to make mistakes

Turf: A specific neighborhood or area held by a specific gang

Up on it: Having knowledge of the drug scene, who's dealing, and so on

V-Code: Gang regulations, with punishment for disobedience

Varrio: *see* Barrio (used by Hispanic gangs)

Vato: Dude (used by Hispanic gangs)

Vato loco: The craziest, most feared Chicano gang member (used by Hispanic gangs)

Veteranos: Older gang members who are now role models for the younger members (used by Hispanic gangs)

Vicky Lous: A derogatory name for Vice Lords (used by Disciples)

Violation: Breaking a gang rule

V-Out: To leave a gang, usually after being beaten by fellow gang members

Wacha: Watch out

Wack: PCP; to kill someone

Wacked: High on PCP; killed by someone

Wanna-be: A person who wants to be a gang member

What it B like?: A Blood greeting

What it C like?: A Crip greeting

What set you from?: Which gang are you affiliated with? (used primarily in California)

What up?: What's happening? A greeting, or a challenge

What up G?: A gangster greeting

Wilding: A gang assault; the beating of a rival gang member

Word: Okay, it's all right

Yierba: Marijuana (used by Hispanic gangs)

Yim jai: A snitch (used by Asian gangs)

Y'que?: What are you going to do? (challenge used by Hispanic gangs)

Zapped: Killed

Zort: Money

NUMBER CODES

Numbers play a very important role in the communication between gangs and gang members. In graffiti, they can represent the area of the city a gang is from, or even a specific street. For example, the number 13 signifies that a gang is from Southern California. A second number could be placed in front of this, followed by a letter or series of letters. 52-BGC-13, then, would represent the 52 Broadway Gangster Crips from southern California.

Numbers are frequently used as warnings to rival gangs. In California, the penal code for murder is 187. When Californian gangs deface other gangs' graffiti, not only will they write their own symbols over it, but they may include the number 187 as well, meaning death to the opposing gang.

A number can also represent a specific letter of the alphabet, or a word beginning with a specific letter. For example, the letter A is the first letter in the alphabet and receives the number 1, the letter P is the sixteenth letter and receives the number 16, and so forth. Put together, the numbers can be arranged to make a statement.

1-9-23	All Is Well (People Nation greeting)
2-7-4-14	Black Gangster Disciple Nation
4-20-1-3	Death To All Crips
21-23-19	United We Stand

The following list of number codes is not all inclusive. Keep in mind that gangs in different parts of the country use different numbers to mean different things. Parents should check their local law enforcement agencies for up-to-date number identification.

Number	Letter	Possible Meaning
1	A	All, Allah, And
2	B	Brotherhood, Black, Boys, Born, Blood
3	C	Crip, See, Cobra
4	D	Death, Disciple, Dragon, Dishonor
5	E	Equal, Equity, East
6	F	Folks, Father
7	G	Gangster, God
8	H	Her, He
9	I	Inca, Islam, Is
10	J	Justice
11	K	Knowledge, Kill, Kingdom
12	L	Latin, Love, Leave, Life, Libre
13	M	Much, Man, Master
14	N	Nation
15	O	One, Of
16	P	Power, People
17	Q	Queen, Quality
18	R	Rifa, Righteous, Ruler, Rules
19	S	Stand, Self, Savior, Sons, Set, Struggle
20	T	Truth, To, The, True, Turf
21	U	Unity, United, Understanding, Universe
22	V	Vato, Victory
23	W	With, We, Wisdom, Win, Wacha,Well
24	X	Unknown
25	Y	You, Why
26	Z	Easy, Zig, Zag

There are some numbers that have other meanings as well:

187	The California state penal code for murder
40	Forty ounces of beer
13	Southern California (used by Hispanic gangs)
14	Northern California (used by Hispanic gangs)
5-0	Five-0, Police
5	Five-point star
6	Six-point star

Appendix Three

NATIONAL DIRECTORY OF RESOURCES

Adolescent Wellness Program
1010 Massachusetts Ave., 2nd Floor
Boston, MA 02118
(617) 534-5196

Offers gang and drug prevention programs, as well as a violence prevention program for teachers. Publishes *Against The Tide,* a bi-monthly newsletter.

California Youth Authority Gang Violence Reduction Project
2445 N. Mariondale Ave., Suite 202
Los Angeles, CA 90032
(213) 227-4114

Operated by parole agents from the state of California. Publishes informational pamphlets as well as a directory of organizations concerned with gangs. Coordinates parenting groups and speaks to other organizations about gang prevention.

Gang Prevention through Targeted Outreach
Boys and Girls Clubs of America
1230 W. Peachtree St. NW
Atlanta, GA 30309-3494
(404) 815-5763/64

A comprehensive program that directs at-risk youths to positive alternatives offered by Boys and Girls Clubs. Uses a referral network involving schools, courts, juvenile justice agencies, social service agencies, police, and community organizations.

Mothers Against Gangs (MAG)
P.O. Box 392
Palatine, IL 60078
(847) 934-0105
Contact: Ms. Diane Pignato

A nationwide organization that utilizes grassroots efforts to educate the community, develop court advocacy, and provide support to families and youths affected by gangs.

Mothers Against Violence
154 Christopher St., 2nd Floor
New York, NY 10014
(212) 255-8484

A coalition of New York City women who work to organize residents, public officials, schools, professionals, and youths to address the violence that's claiming hundreds of children annually.

National Council on Crime and Delinquency
685 Market St., Suite 620
San Francisco, CA 94105
(415) 896-6223
Dr. Barry Krisberg, President

Aims crime prevention programs at at-risk youths, offering family intervention and assistance for low-income youths, and focusing on youths who drop out of school. Offers a quarterly journal, *Crime and Delinquency,* as well as other papers for schools and organizations.

National Crime Prevention Council
1700 K St. N.W., 2nd Floor
Washington, DC 20006-3817
Phone (202) 466-6272
Fax (202) 296-1356

Provides training and programs to individuals and groups interested in crime prevention. Publishes the newsletter *Catalyst* ten times a year. Created the popular "McGruff" program—"Take a Bite Out of Crime."

National Institute of Justice
P.O. Box 6000
Rockville, MD 20849-6000
(800) 851-3420

The primary federal sponsor for research on crime—its prevention and control. Offers an extensive bibliography. Many of its publications are available free of charge or at a nominal cost.

National Youth Gang Center
Office of Juvenile Justice and Delinquency Prevention
P.O. Box 12729
Tallahassee, FL 32317
Phone (904) 385-0600
Fax (904) 386-5356
Contact: Donna J. Lindquist

Assists state and local governments in the collection, analysis, and exchange of information on gang-related demographics, legislation, literature, research, and promising program strategies. Coordinates activities with the OJJDP Gang Consortium—a group of federal agencies, gang program representatives, and service providers.

Ten Point Coalition
215 Forest Hills St.
Jamaica Plain, MA 02130
(617) 524-4331

An ecumenical group of Christian clergy and lay leaders working to engage the community with issues affecting at-risk black youths. Provides technical assistance, resource development, training, and networking opportunities for churches and other organizations interested in mentoring, advocacy, economic alternatives, and violence prevention for young people.

NOTES

1. James Haskins, *Street Gangs Yesterday and Today* (New York: Hastings House Publishers, 1974), p. 27.
2. Ibid., p. 28.
3. Ibid., pp. 27, 31.
4. Leòn Bing, *Do or Die* (New York: HarperCollins, 1991), pp. 149-150.

BIBLIOGRAPHY AND READING LIST

Bing, Leòn. *Do or Die.* New York: HarperCollins, 1991.

Blau, Robert, and David Jackson. "Jewelry to Die For." *Chicago Tribune,* 22 June 1993.

Christensen, Loren. *Skinhead Street Gangs.* Boulder, CO: Paladin, 1994.

Conly, Catherine H. *Street Gangs: Current Knowledge and Strategies.* Prepared for the National Institute of Justice, U.S. Department of Justice. August 1992.

Connell, Rich, and Robert J. Lopez, "An Inside Look at 18th Street's Menace." *Los Angeles Times.* 17 November 1996.

Cruz, Nicky. *Code Blue: Urgent Care for the American Youth Emergency.* Ann Arbor, MI: Servane Publications, 1995.

———. *Run Baby Run.* Plainfield, NJ: Logos International, 1968.

Haskins, James. *Street Gangs Yesterday and Today.* New York: Hastings House Publishers, 1974.

Huff, Ronald C., and Arnold P. Goldstein, eds. *The Gang Intervention Handbook*. Champaign, IL: Research Press, 1993.

Karuhn, Carri. "Codes Help Pupils Dress for Success." *Chicago Tribune*. 26 September 1996.

Korem, Daniel J. *Suburban Gangs—The Affluent Rebels*. Richardson, TX: International Focus Press, 1994.

———. *Suburban Gang Update*. Richardson, TX: International Focus Press, 1996.

Office of Juvenile Justice and Delinquency Prevention. *Gang Suppression and Intervention: Problem and Response Research Summary*. Washington, D.C.: 1994.

Operation Safe Streets (OSS) Street Gang Detail. *"L.A. Style": A Street Gang Manual of the Los Angeles County Sheriff's Department*. Los Angeles: November 1994.

Teen Angels Magazine. No. 133. Rialto, CA.

"Three More Jailed in Attack on Deaf Man." *Minneapolis Star Tribune*. 10 March 1995.

Todd, Susan, and Andrew Young, prods. and dirs. *Lives in Hazard*. 57 min. Olmos Productions: 1993. Videocassette.

Underground 'Zine. *Rap Pages*. No. 18. February 1996.

READING LIST

Nonfiction Books

Juvenile and Young Adult

Gardner, Sandra. *Street Gangs In America.* New York: Franklin Watts, 1992.

Greenberg, Keith Elliot. *Out of the Gang.* Minneapolis: Lerner Publications, 1992.

Oliver, Marilyn Tower. *Gangs: Trouble in the Streets.* Springfield, N.J.: Enslow Publishers, 1995.

Rosen, Roger, and Patra McSharry, eds. *Street Gangs: Gaining Turf, Losing Ground.* New York: Rosen Publishing Group, 1991.

Webb, Margo. *Coping with Street Gangs.* New York: Rosen Publishing Group, 1990.

Adult

Arthur, Richard, with Edsel Erickson. *Gangs and Schools.* Holmes Beach, FL: Learning Publications, 1992.

Campbell, Anne. *The Girls in the Gang.* 2nd ed. Cambridge, MA.: Blackwell, 1991.

Hinojosa, Maria. *Crews: Gang Members Talk to Maria Hinojosa*. San Diego: Harcourt Brace, 1995.

Jankowski, Martin. *Islands in the Street: Gangs and Urban American Society*. Berkeley: University of California Press, 1991.

Klein, Malcolm. *The American Street Gang: Its Nature, Prevalence and Control*. New York: Oxford University Press, 1995.

———. *The Modern Gang Reader.* Los Angeles: Roxbury Publishing Company, 1995.

Korem, Daniel J. *Streetwise Parents, Foolproof Kids*. 2nd rev. ed. Richardson, Texas: International Focus Press, 1995.

Moore, Joan W. *Going Down to the Barrio: Homeboys and Homegirls in Change*. Philadelphia: Temple University Press, 1991.

Padilla, Felix M. *The Gang as an American Enterprise*. New Brunswick, N.J.: Rutgers University Press, 1992.

Rodriguez, Luis J. *Always Running: La Vida Loca: Gang Days in L.A.* Willimantic, CO: Curbstone, 1993.

Shakur, Sanika. *Monster: The Autobiography of an L.A. Gang Member.* New York: Penguin, 1994.

Fiction

Adult

Mowry, Jess. *Way Past Cool.* New York: Farrar, Straus and Giroux, 1992.

McConnell, Christopher. *A Nation of Amor.* Sag Harbor, NY: Permanent Press, 1994.

Wright, Richard. *Rite of Passage.* New York: Harper Collins, 1994.

Juvenile and Young Adult

Hinton, S. E. *The Outsiders.* New York: Viking Press, 1967.

———. *Rumble Fish.* New York: Delecorte Press, 1976.

Hopper, Nancy J. *The Truth or Dare Trap.* New York: Dutton, 1985.

Meyers, Walter D. *Scorpions.* New York: Harper and Row, 1988.

Peterson, P. J. *Nobody Else Can Walk It for You.* New York: Delecorte Press, 1982.

WORD INDEX

GANG NAME INDEX

NOTES

Photograph by Lindsay Sachs

Steven L. Sachs lives in Illinois with his wife and daughter. He has been an officer of the Nineteenth Judicial Circuit of Lake County for over eighteen years, serving as a juvenile probation officer, juvenile detentions counselor, home detention officer, and pretrial bond supervision officer.